Collected Essays
of
Gary Beck

To those who recognize America for what it is and
want it to be better.

Essays from The Collected Essays of Gary Beck have appeared in:

63 Channels, AIM Magazine, Bergen Street Review, Banango Street, Bedford (St. Martins Press), Bewildering Stories, Blue Lake Review, Campbell Corners Language Exchange, CC & D Magazine, C.L.A. Journal, Consciousness: Literature and the Arts, Down in the Dirt Magazine (Scars Publications), Elimae, Fear of Monkeys (Twin Enterprises), Fine Lines, Gently Read Literature, Geronimo Review, Greensburg Magazine, Hemingway's Shotgun, Ink Pantry (Ink Pantry Publishing), International Zeitschrift, Ipod Buffet, Lit Up Magazine, Loquacious Placemat (Twisted Thistle Productions), Lunar Poetry, Nazar Look, Ontologica Magazine, Outcry Magazine, Penniless Press, Plum Ruby Review, Poetic Matrix Press, Poor Mojo Almanack, PPP Ezine (Poetry, Poetics and Pleasure), Purple Dream, Record Magazine, Section 8 Magazine, Setu, Shanti Art/Stillpoint Quarterly, Shelf Life Magazine, Slurve Magazine, Sorrowland Press, Straitjacket Magazine, The Chicago Record, The Dramatists Guild Quarterly, The Oracular Tree, The Papermachine, The Recusant, The Shine Journal, The Straitjackets Magazine, The Wimpole Street Gazette, The Wolfian, Verbal Art (Authors Press), We Feel Pretty, Weasel Press, Wimpole Street Gazette, Wolf Moon Journal, Writing Raw

Introduction

It was very refreshing to read this collection of essays, by Gary Beck, which range from the 1970's through the present time. The essays are undated, but it's not difficult to date them based on their content and historical references. I use the word refreshing literally, because of his approaches to these issues still with us, despite new forms or names and new technology.

His approach is refreshing because its methodology is, generally speaking, both abstract-concrete, and, generally speaking, eschews a right or a left slant as oversimplification. Rather, he uses reason and history, to support his positions, and sometimes, with a clever use of irony, too, as in his essay 'Why We Don't Need Background Checks to Purchase Guns'. The essays deal with such socially relevant themes as the distribution of wealth in society, homelessness, prisons, government accountability and corporate greed vs social responsibility, and the 2008 mortgage crisis. I thought the first two essays, on alleviating homelessness and improving the situation for prisoners, were particularly comprehensive, as well as the essay, Republic of Dreams, for its overview of society, also "Social Speculation" and "Fairness Manifesto" for their conciseness and originality.

Of particular note, is the author's advice on education, both for adults, and in the school, concerning the relevance of art, to the individual's quality of life, and art's social value. To this, he brings a lifetime of experience as a producer, and director of both classical and modern theatre, and as a playwright and author of fiction and poetry. So, for instance, he advises theatre and classics departments to collaborate, not compete, and stresses the importance of music education, i.e. teaching students the ability to listen to and understand classical music. There are also essays on art education. .

Once heralded as a democratizing institution, the internet, in particular, he writes, has merely become a manifestation of circus, to divert the people from vital issues. He encourages original approaches to literary themes. He includes an essay which makes a penetrating case for a non-conventional interpretation of Hamlet as being resolute rather than irresolute in Shakespeare's play. He also reflects on the role and relevance of comic art, and of the role the clown as social critic. He also supports the restoration of poetry as a pre-eminent art-form, as it was in classical Greece. He also emphasizes the ability of poetry to address social issues, and not just delve into subjective and emotional states, which he describes as a dominant theme in current poetry.

In Beck's interesting eclectic mix of positions, he decries corporate elitism, and defends the right of the poor and downtrodden against the rich and powerful — arguments associated with the political Left.

Given his sympathy for educationally deprived children, the homeless and prisoners, and the economically deprived, why is the author so hard on illegal immigrants, whom he refers to by the emotionally laden term, favored by the Right-wing, as "illegal aliens"?. (see *The American Burden*). Beck sees the presence of illegal immigrants in the US, as raising, and then violating, the issue of national sovereignty, or the right of a nation to choose people, to admit or exclude within its borders, or accept as possible citizens. Those who come illegally, violate the border and deserve to be excluded, he argues. His justification is the famous Treaty of Westphalia in 1648, which ended the 30 Year War in Europe, and established the concept of national sovereignty.

Dealing with suffering as a human rights issue, is, by way of contrast, part of his approach to suffering and the issue of inequality in America. For instance, he views letting failing schools continue to exist as a Constitutional violation……(*That our society allows these conditions to go on year after year in*)……. *a violation of individual rights guaranteed by the Constitution of the United States amounts to crimes against humanity. Whatever the failings of the parents, the children should not be abandoned to a devastating existence in the present and dismal prospects for the future.*

Beck also recognizes fairness, as a real issue, and not just as an abstraction, in his essay, "The Fairness Manifesto." He writes: ... *Our system is even more corrupt than ancient Rome, where class distinction was endemic, since our society deceives with lofty ideals of the constitution, limited to the benefit of the few. The constitution is suspended for a single mother with children living in a homeless shelter. Here we feed the hungry on myths of equality. He has an interesting solution too, in the same essay, creation of a political party called The Fairness Party: All Americans should have the opportunity through education and effort to better their lives. A new political entity, 'The Fairness Party', dedicated to abating the selfish tyranny of excessive wealth, should be founded. The member's first commitment will be to request legislation that allows a fair chance for all to participate in the American dream.*

One could argue that these human rights should apply to illegal immigrants too, many of whom seek refuge here because social anarchy at home makes ordinary life impossible. Those sent back because they arrived illegally to an almost certain doomed fate, are as those in boats, sometimes sinking boats who also seek refuge. Should they be permitted to drown, and not be rescued?

The issue of state power vs. human rights is a prominent theme in one of the essays that Beck presents here, the essay on Antigone. She is ordered by the King to not bury her brother, who is regarded as a traitor. But she believes that she has a higher human-divine duty to bury him. She does, and she is executed by the King. Are not the rights described in the US Constitution– rights of life, liberty and pursuit of happiness – basic human rights? That's why immigrants come here, and why the country has been a beacon for the oppressed, a State of Liberty among nations. Pragmatically speaking, no one nation ought to bear responsibility for immigration problems in the world, which is one of the reasons the United Nations exists, as well as to prevent war among nations, a theme of Beck's, to which we'll return shortly.

To this interesting mix of left-right positions, we might add Beck's views on education and its role in leadership. We've already seen one very practical result of his focus on the importance of education, namely his call for a Fairness Party to alleviate the disparities caused by major divisions of wealth. However, he also calls for cultivation of an educated, informed leadership class composed of individuals who are not part of the apparatus of globalism and corporate control, who would problem-solve within the context of what is most beneficial for humanity, and the planet as a whole. The position is also reminiscent of Plato's famous Dialogue on a utopian society, *The Republic*, in which people are trained to be leaders, from birth, and act from civic responsibility, not personal gain.

Approaching the results of education in these very practical ways, is a unique feature of this book, and represents a very constructive approach to world problem solving, that I hopes gains a wider audience. To that end, let me cite two paragraphs, from two different essays in the book.

We cannot suppose that our nation is at crossroads. That would presume clear choices. We may be *facing the most perilous time in the history of the republic. A time of industrial, technical, scientific, perhaps even moral decline, that leaves our vulnerable citizens apprehensive, our aware citizens uneasy. Our ailing system indicates that we cannot resurrect obsolete industries and compete in the world market in manufacturing products that are produced cheaper and better abroad. It has not been determined if our advanced technical industries can sustain a nation. The gulf between haves and have-nots keeps widening to the point of creating a de facto oligarchy. It is uncertain if the wounded giant can regenerate itself. We urgently need great leadership to steer us through these ominous pitfalls. New directions and new horizons must be found, before the republic of dreams dwindles to a second world reality.* (from the essay, "Republic of Dreams")

Beck continues on this theme of developing a new, capable non-self-serving group of leaders, world servers, as it were, dedicated to helping humanity, apart from their personal gain.

If the human race is to survive the coming calamities that we have engineered; global warming, depletion of the ozone layer, deforestation, disasters man-made, as well as those imposed by nature, we require a new kind of leadership and new directions in national policy. In a world wracked with poverty, disease, hunger, ethnic hatreds and endless wars, we need wise and skilled guardians, who could try to salvage our planet, before it is too late. The highest priority of the United Nations and all functional first world governments, should be to locate and nurture a new class of leaders, techno-humanists, who might possibly construct the only potential direction for earthly survival. An international academy should be created, recruiting potential candidates worldwide, for service dedicated to civilization's continuation. An independent commission under U.N. auspices would screen applicants for the required technical, conceptual and moral skills mandatory for world guidance. After sufficient preparation, their task would be to reeducate humanity in how to preserve our planet. (Academy curricula and operations plan available on request by designated representatives of heads of state and the U.N.) (from the essay, Social Speculation.)

Collected Essays of Gary Beck is a very worthwhile book by Gary Beck. You will find the book stimulating and well-written, even if you disagree with some of its positions. It will get you thinking, and learning, it may challenge your positions, and help us face, and even solve the most serious challenges of our time.

Paul Dolinsky, PhD
Author of "Philosophy Guide in Verse
August 2018

Contents

Crisis in the Classics

There is a great theatrical need for readable and performable drama for students, scholars and theatergoers. The standard translations of the classics, first read in Classics 101, were derived from great Victorian and Edwardian scholars, who represented a very different audience and language from post-Vietnam America. Their scholarship was vast and may have intimidated subsequent scholars, some of whom were eager to present American styles. But they were uncertain how to disassemble the Homeric but ponderous literary forms that were beginning to alienate modern readers.

Translators concerned with the theatre reacted to the traditional sonorous renderings of Aeschylus and Sophocles with enthusiastic updatings, that frequently located gods and heroes in the Okefenokee swamps, a bar, or an inner city ghetto. This patronizing innovation of arbitrarily updating for modern audiences reduced the soaring greatness of the Greek drama. Fewer and fewer people were moved by the works that had thrilled western man, from the 5th century B.C., until 21st century 'easy access'. Since it is much more demanding to attend a theater performance than to read the book, theater must make greater efforts to reach audiences already disillusioned with the classics.

Today, by its very nature, there is an elitism inherent in the classics, since the normal venues are the classroom and theater. This will expose the privileged class to the great ethical, intellectual and cultural issues of the classics, but not make them readily available to the vast majority of highly intelligent, but not so well educated American audiences. The classics should never be exclusionary. They can light creative fires in anyone. They should be available to everyone who can appreciate the scope of their grandeur, passion, nobility, arrogance, stubbornness and pettiness.

Unlike in ages past, today a book or theater performance must compete with an almost endless menu of diversions. However potent the material, it reaches a smaller audience than the New York Yankees, or Batman movies. But the Yankees and Batman may not endure the test of time as well as Aeschylus and Sophocles. The Greek drama is not a low cognitive activity, easily grasped. It is a profound experience that can potentially dazzle anyone with the wonder and brilliance of the human mind, as portrayed in the earliest and greatest expression of dramatic literature. Yet the drama requires effort and involvement from the reader or theatergoer, so they can glean the rich rewards from the extremes of comedy and tragedy.

Students who read classical drama shouldn't have to trudge through the chores of stilted or deconstructed language in order to appreciate the grand issues and wonderful stories. The elements should be harmonious. Greek is one of the great languages of heroic poetry, as is English, so it is unacceptable for English translations to inhibit the use of imagination, and curtail the feeling of pleasure derived from immortal plays. First and foremost, a play must be readable. If someone can't enjoy reading Aristophanes, they certainly won't go to see his plays performed. This premise defines the need for accessible texts, that maintain their integrity. The 'classics are heavy' syndrome is inaccurate. We simply require an exciting text to shatter that misconception.

Today, instructors of the classics are as well prepared for their students, as well educated in general and as dynamic as teachers past. Yet they are more hindered by their archaic material, which is often difficult for their students to master. However dedicated the instructor, commitment cannot overcome the burden of language that renders a classic uninteresting or unappealing to an intelligent student. Students should be well-educated in the humanities. Yet the classics seem to be a declining factor in contemporary education, at a time when our society has great need of consideration of the moral issues that the classics present.

Our classics classrooms should be crowded with students, eager to intellectually grapple with the eternal problems that confront us. Instead, diminishing enrollments jeopardize the widespread dissemination of classical learning. We can't condescend to bright minds with plays whose dialect and idiobabble confuse or demean great literature. That is as destructive as stultifying versification. We must clarify the language of translation so these wondrous works will thrill and delight readers. Instructors shouldn't be perceived as curators of dreary literary relics. They should be appreciated as purveyors of tools from the exciting past, that relate to the present and could help us better deal with the future.

Current performance styles create a confusing arena for the classical drama. College drama departments generally encourage students to approach the Greek classics in one of two basic formats: A museum like reproduction, with turgid production elements, totally out of touch with the theatergoers, such as unison chanting choruses, rigid prose, stylized movement, and droning poetic recitation; or alternatively, arbitrary updating, with complete removal of the grandiose ethics and passions, rejection of the moral debate which is the substance of the Greek drama, and the critical fault of making every character socially equal, until class and moral distinctions blend into an amorphous mass of confused theatrical values, expressed as 'you guys'.

Drama became the exclusive province of the university as the training ground for professional theater in the 1970's. This was a by-product of the emergence of regional theaters, affiliated with universities. The nature of this custodianship of theater is still evolving. The need is great for theater departments to include the classics departments as collaborators or consultants in play production, since theater professors are neither historians or cultural scholars. This would facilitate exploring the complexities of Greek drama and result in more meaningful performances. This may require diplomatic and conflict resolution skills, since theater departments frequently treat the Greek classics like any other period, while their major concern is with the Elizabethans and moderns. This is a natural occurrence, since these periods are of more current interest to students, due to easier access in reading and the ready availability of numerous theater productions. Thus the unique differences between the Greek drama, which was a state-approved, social, religious, political and dramatic spectacle, perhaps historically closer in significance to a combination of a church mass and an election rally, are not treated differently than a Broadway musical, or a National Endowment for the Arts funded production in the not-for-profit theater.

The lack of theater commitment to the unique integrity of the Greek drama authorizes directors to deconstruct the classics and rebuild them, however they choose. Although this may sometimes allow interesting flights of fancy in individual creative expression, other values are neglected. Audiences quickly weary of Lysistrata protesting panty raids in a college dormitory, or Agamemnon as a Mafia Boss, strutting around a bar, buying drinks for the house to celebrate his victory over Troy.

It is necessary to reignite the interest of readers and theatergoers to the value of the classics, lest they be lost to future audiences. The Greek drama potentially offers an emotional rollercoaster ride, first rate entertainment, eternal human values and the richest body of extant ancient literature. This is a heady combination that must harness all the component elements of the plays, in order to reach and fulfill the audiences of today, as well as tomorrow. All we have to do is spur a neo-renaissance in the classics.

Not Your Every Day Homeless Proposal

Homelessness has become a persistent problem in urban environments and multiplies rapidly in the periods of economic downturn that follow cycles of prosperity. In New York City, for example, recognized by some as the homeless capitol of the world, the dim economic forecast through at least the year 2007 makes it exceedingly improbable that there will be additional funds to alleviate the resurgent homeless situation. Families with children are entering the homeless system in record numbers that have surpassed even the dreadful surge of homelessness during the Koch administration in the 1980's. Regardless of the reasons that homeless families enter the shelter system, they should be accorded the highest priority of attention, because children are the group most vulnerable to the pernicious effects of homelessness. There is a moral and constitutional duty to insure that homeless children, who are the victims rather than the cause of their family's plight, will have a chance for education, happiness and an opportunity to obtain a piece of the mythical American dream.

Too often in New York City there is an ongoing struggle between not-for-profit advocacy groups and the Department of Homeless Services, regarding issues related to intake, shelter and services for the homeless. Without the efforts of the non-government organizations the shelter system would be in even more dismal shape. Not every city has a staunch defender of the rights of the homeless like Justice Helen E. Freedman of the New York State Supreme Court. She has played a major role in shaping the city's policies for the homeless, with particular concern for the treatment of families with children. Despite all efforts by government and the private sector, the situation of the homeless remains perilous. Successive New York City administrations have continued to house homeless families in deteriorated and dangerous welfare hotels and motels, rife with drugs, prostitution and violence, that are the children's learning curricula in these unchartered crime academys.

Since it is an acknowledged fact that cities cannot afford to build a sufficiency of low-income housing with concomitant support services for the homeless, other options should be explored. A New York City proposal to house the homeless in an abandoned prison showed a typical government insensitivity to this population group. If the city first announced that they planned to convert the facility to a suitable residential structure, it might have been favorably received. Instead, it appeared that the government was going to put the homeless in jail. Another proposal that must have been intended to entertain the public, rather than offer a serious solution, was a plan to place homeless families on refitted cruise ships, to be anchored in New York Harbor. The New York City Commissioner of Homeless Services actually made a visit to the Bahamas, purportedly to inspect unused cruise ships. The safety, security and supervisory considerations that would be necessary for shipboard dwelling should have led to instant rejection of the plan, by whomever it was first suggested to. Of course any resemblance to British prison hulks in the Revolutionary War that stored inconvenient bodies was strictly coincidental.

When the homeless problem became a major embarrassment to the Koch administration in the mid-eighties, homeless families were placed in decrepit midtown Manhattan hotels, where no tourists in their right minds would have conceived of spending even one night. These hotels could not previously rent rooms for $29.00 per night. Suddenly they were billing the city $100.00 per night, for warehousing families with children in the heart of mid-town Manhattan. There was no apparent government concern that the hotels were far from supermarkets, laundries, childrens playgrounds and other community services necessary for the daily functioning of families. The tiny hotel rooms, barely large enough for one person, hadn't been painted for years. There were no cooking facilities, a frequent lack of heat in winter and often no hot water all year round. The insect and rodent infested rooms were completely inadequate to shelter families. Crime, drugs, prostitution and violence thrived in the isolated confines of an environment that was totally unsuitable for children.

The Guiliani administration in the 'nineties' cunningly moved much of the homeless population to hotels and motels in the outer boroughs. Yet they still paid at least as much or more for rooms, then the Koch administration had for traditionally more expensive rooms in Manhattan. The Guiliani administration astutely recognized that the media would only leave the comforts of Manhattan Island for major stories such as murder, arson, etc. They knew there was no glamour in the outer boroughs. There was also a cynical awareness that the media would be reluctant to investigate the ongoing problems of a social group that lacks political clout, despite the human suffering, because the homeless don't vote and consequently are not part of a constituency that has legislators to defend their interests. The homeless are represented by what has become a small but vocal not-for-profit industry, that in turn is dependent on the homeless for its existence. The relationship between the Guiliani administration and homeless advocates was frequently contentious, to the detriment of the homeless, who were in desperate need of services. The Bloomberg administration continues to house the homeless in tawdry hotels and motels at the cost of $3,500.00 to $4,500.00 per month, for rooms that most people would deem uninhabitable.

The cost of rooms to house the homeless is only part of the expenditures on this dependent population. Outrageous housing costs have been justified over the years by the assertion that designated federal funds will only pay for temporary housing. An active New York State Congressional delegation could most probably arrange a small alternate funding stream, for longer term housing solutions. Another infliction on the homeless was that the Guiliani administration rigorously enforced arbitrary rules that allowed them to exclude needy petitioners from entering the homeless system. The reason given was the administration's fear that the working poor would flood the shelter system as a route for attaining better housing. It was beyond the capacity of the Guiliani administration to address the needs of the working poor. Therefore, a convoluted mechanism to avoid the issue was contrived; emergency funds for temporary housing only, however extravagant the cost of the rentals. We are confronted with a peculiar dysfunction when the government pays upper middle class rental rates, for accommodations below slum standards.

There are no simple solutions for this desperate situation that devours the futures of hundreds of youth annually. The real problem is society's lack of will to urgently address an issue that should have been resolved in the 19th century; cooperation between the government and the private sector to provide solutions for the problems of the needy. There is an overwhelming need to develop innovative plans that will concentrate efforts on alleviating the burdens of homelessness on the most fragile group, families with children. One possible plan would target economically depressed communities using upstate New York as an example, that are struggling to remain solvent and functional. This could be a model for other areas of the country. Depressed communities face a grim future, with little hope of the arrival of new industries that will replace lost blue collar and farm jobs. Certain qualifying communities could be offered a partnership with select pioneer homeless families, in a venture that could benefit both groups.

Appropriate towns that have an infrastructure of schools, transportation, medical services, grocery stores, laundromats and most important, a civic system capable of problem solving would be identified. They would be approached by designated personnel who would present a proposal that would demonstrate the economic benefits to the towns for providing residential sites and a supportive environment for designated homeless families. Abandoned property would be leased, reactivating the tax base for the towns. Renovation of the properties would stimulate local employment and generate earnings for businesses that sell construction materials and supplies. Support services for the families would develop new jobs that would infuse cash in the towns. Some jobs, after negotiations with the towns, would be reserved for the new residents. Living expenses of the families would directly contribute cash to the local economies.

Suitable families would be recruited for 'small town pioneering' after a careful selection and preparation process. The first requirement would be functionality. The mentally ill homeless would not be an appropriate target group. But at least 25% to 30% of homeless families are functional, many having fallen into the system because of economic disaster like loss of job, or a fire that destroyed home or apartment, etc. The benefits of small town life would be presented as a positive alternative to the stress of urban shelters and poverty communities. The families would have to be prepared to adapt to a new and unaccustomed environment. The towns would also need preparation to receive a new population group as welcome neighbors. Job development for both town residents and the newcomer families would be a priority.

The small town pioneering program would start as a pilot project. Appropriate personnel would be assigned to contact potentially qualified towns. Ten towns would be chosen to house ten families each, for a total of one hundred families. Questionnaires should be developed in cooperation with NGO's and the Departments of Homeless Services to identify qualified families, willing to undergo a major change in their way of life. Funds required for the initial phase of the project, outreach to the designated towns and families are minimal. If funds are not available from the Department of Homeless Services, or other concerned government agencies, they would be solicited from private foundations. Once towns and families have been selected, project activities would commence simultaneously in the towns and the homeless shelters.

The towns should identify suitable residential space, preferably one- or two-family homes that have been underutilized or abandoned, that would then be renovated for habitation. Assisted living services would be identified and organized. Social workers, one per town, each to manage a caseload of ten families, would be recruited, with incentives offered to induce them to live in the community. Budgets for living expenses would be prepared. Training for the families in small town living skills would be followed by orientation tours of the intended communities. There would be introductions to the local residents: shopkeepers, teachers, town officials, neighbors, etc. The families and towns respectively should be prepared to fulfill their obligations to each other. The nearest colleges should be invited to participate in the project and provide educational services, as well as job or career training.

Funding for this demonstration program would be requested from the New York State legislature, various federal agencies, the New York City Department of Homeless Services, the office of the Mayor of New York City, private foundations and corporations. Small town pioneering should be developed as a model program that would be replicable, after an appropriate demonstration period. The relatively low start up cost per family, as well as proportionately low operating costs, would be far less then the cost of housing a family in a temporary shelter. This would make it possible to run the program for far less than the cost to maintain a family in a shelter, which is approximately $45,000 annually, for a family of three. The savings to the taxpayer would be considerable and the benefits to both towns and families would be immense.

Concerned officials, agencies and NGO's should consider this program as a possible amelioration to the problem of homelessness for a substantial number of families capable of rebuilding their future. This proposal is presented as only one possible solution to a major problem for which many new initiatives are needed. Other programs that could be explored might include: the development of co-operative apartment houses; an urban pioneering initiative utilizing abandoned buildings in poverty neighborhoods, for reclamation as housing stock; perhaps a more daring venture in commune/kibbutz experiments. Hopefully, these suggestions will stimulate consideration by those concerned with the future well-being of neglected members of our society, of the urgent need for new, practical solutions for the problems of homeless families with children.

Imprisoning America

The many drastic problems confronting our democratic land often distract us from examining prisons in America. The system currently contains approximately 1,200,000 inmates, a number larger than the population of several countries. The laws that were passed to determine prison sentences for crimes were not created by wise men or women, but legislators, beholden to special interests, certain ideological positions, or ignorance of the nature of justice.

The sterile, non-productive industry, at prodigious taxpayer expense, employs legions of workers, whose primary purpose is to continue stable confinement of the inmates in hundreds of penal institutions. The increasing trend for privatization of the penal system may offer a modicum of economic relief to an over-burdened government, but it changes the nature and purpose of imprisonment. Except for lifers, with no possibility of parole, each inmate has been sentenced to a period of confinement, that could be shortened by qualifying behavior. A private prison enterprise, paid by the government, must have a sufficiency of inmates to make a profit. It will not willingly give up its bread and butter components.

Historically, the prison system has been a nurturing ground for furthering criminal activity upon release, because of two basic circumstances; the inmate is rarely prepared to pursue an alternative to criminal activity, and is invariably returned to the same environment that facilitated the criminal activity that brought this person into the system. The social phenomenon that once saw the prison population made up of primarily white males, has evolved to multi-cultural, with ethnic minorities, mostly from poverty communities, making up a majority of those confined..

It is painfully obvious that imprisonment neither prevents crime, nor alters the mindset of criminals. Both judicial and social change is necessary to amend the ineffective, non-productive storage system that only comes to the general attention of the public in the event of an infrequent inmate riot or inquiry about a scandal. Non-violent offenders should be the first group targeted for a new approach. They should be thoroughly educated to understand the curse of recidivism. They should be offered life skills and work studies training, in preparation for alternative employment to flipping burgers. Supervised housing in transitional communities would keep the parolee from the neighborhood and friends that originally involved him in crime. Intense social and other services will be less expensive then the cost of long term confinement. The real question is will our nation have the nerve to change an unproductive system, that employs many thousands, whose jobs are protected by legislators, Federal and state.

Hamlet, The Misperceived Prince

Hamlet has been severely chastised for hundreds of years by scholars, theater directors and critics for his indecision and lack of resolution. The legions of absolutely certain authorities have thoroughly convinced the small number of the classical drama attending public and the slightly larger readership of serious drama that the young prince is unable to take action. As is typical of much of literary criticism, the critics are frequently more intent on enhancing themselves, while belittling the accomplishments of someone else. Prince Hamlet, arguably the most complex character in all drama, in arguably the greatest play in all drama, is tragically misunderstood.

There are elements of the play that have not been sufficiently explored by the academic authorities who are the primary interpreters of literature. For example: Denmark is a powerful kingdom in a time of ongoing struggle for dominance among rival countries. The king of Denmark is a strong monarch who exerts enormous influence on his neighbors and vassals, militarily and diplomatically, as far away as England. Yet when Hamlet the king dies, and his brother Claudius quickly marries his widow and ascends the throne, there is no apparent disruption of government, or opposition to the regime change.

There is no information in the play about the Danish laws of succession to the throne, but Claudius' accession is obviously reasonably acceptable as a fait accompli, since there is no resistance from popular or special interests. Prince Hamlet harbors many strong feelings about current events; the death of his father, the hasty marriage of his recently widowed mother, the pomp and ceremony of the new king, but he gives no indication that his inheritance has been stolen, or that he plans rebellion. Power resides in the hands of his uncle, and Hamlet has no following of powerful magnates, or influential courtiers to support any claim he may have to the throne.

Except for Horatio, who he had almost forgotten, and some casual acquaintances among the soldiers in Elsinore, Hamlet is completely isolated. As a prince of a great house, well educated by contemporary standards, Hamlet is fully aware of the politics of his situation. He has no influence, no adherents, no friends in a royal court just recently established that is jealous of its prerogatives, not yet secure in rulership, yet resolved to exercise power. Hamlet has been shunted aside, while an uncle, whose earlier relationship with him has not been explicated, rules the kingdom. We have not been informed about Prince Hamlet's expectations when his father was alive. It is reasonable to assume that as a sophisticated prince he must have anticipated that he would become king upon his father's death, which he certainly didn't expect to occur so soon.

The confrontation with the ghost of his father changes everything for Hamlet, but alters nothing in his circumstances. He is still alone and he dare not confide in anyone. He has no proof of murder, except for the word of a ghost, which enflames him with horror and outrage. But the ghost provides no assistance, only a call for vengeance. When Hamlet pretends to be mad to conceal his purpose, he reveals the poverty of his means to do anything overtly to redress the current situation. He trusts no one, just as any prince of a royal house would trust no one when a throne is at stake. Once Hamlet accepts the word of the ghost, he realizes that he is in a Medici-like court, full of poisonous intrigue, but he is not a low, brutal assassin, so he will not rush beserkly on the usurper and hack him to death.

The only resources Hamlet has to redress a great wrong are his sovereign reason and possibly Horatio. He is woefully ill-equipped to dethrone a king, but resolutely determined to take action. He immediately decides that he can no longer afford the risks of vulnerability in his relationship with Ophelia. We are never certain how deep his feelings are for her, but his duty to his murdered father takes priority over any romantic or sexual considerations. He knows that he must confront a ruthless monarch who has committed terrible crimes to obtain a throne, and who must indeed be feared.

It is a most superficial conclusion to assume that Hamlet is indecisive and irresolute. He is a combination of many qualities, human and royal. He fully realizes that it is a daunting undertaking to topple a king. He agonizes over the terrible burden of seeking bloody vengeance. Scholarly commentators may scrutinize the horror of murder and mayhem with too much detachment to appreciate such an intimidating undertaking. It is easy to glibly debase Hamlet with accusations of doubt, inaction, or timidity, when his efforts to carry out a dreadful deed are what make him profoundly human. Despite overwhelming opposition, Hamlet's determination never wavers, which confirms that he is a man of deeds as well as words.

Hamlet is not a vainglorious Bonnie Prince Charlie, consuming his loyal Scots adherents in futile efforts to restore the House of Stuart. He is not, as many critics would seem to prefer, a Jacobean slaughterer, eager to wade through blood to reach the throne. His is an Elizabethan sensibility, set in a northern kingdom that in Shakespeare's depiction is far more Tudor than Nordic. From the moment he pledges the ghost that he will avenge him, he is committed to action. If he hesitates, if he questions his purpose, those doubts only add to the magnitude of his task, thus elevating his stature as a character.

It has conveniently been overlooked that Hamlet is as handy with a sword as he is with his wit. A masterful dramatist has given us much more than a butcher merely programmed to kill. This much maligned Prince is a true tragic hero, without the burden of great flaws, or a curse on his house. His fate has not been pre-determined by any fault of his. He is an innocent victim, who has committed no crime, who is ultimately destroyed by the ambition of another. Let us the more appreciate that Hamlet, by not rushing precipitously to murder Claudius until his evil doing is publicly revealed, allows us to experience the full scope of tragedy.

Repay the People

Not too long ago, we observed anti-war protestor's objections against the war in Iraq facilely segue into anti-occupation activities, which further distracted the American public from a clearer understanding of the political situation. Now protestors are engaged in the current pastime of the traditional majority, lawsuits seeking damages from the government for restricting their protest. Yet while these frivolous legal activities take place, our sons and daughters are still at risk, and their bodies, as well as our national treasure are paying for the war in Iraq. Despite suspicions of the Bush administration's motives for attacking Iraq, the search for weapons of mass destruction will go on. But WMD are only part of the de facto issue; we occupy the country and we have acknowledged that we are accountable to our friends abroad. There must also be a more forthcoming recognition that we are accountable to our citizens at home.

As the anti-war foes slowly submerge into academia, or slink into corporate comforts, they should be reminded to raise their voices in defense of vital domestic needs that have been shortchanged by the war. Granted that it isn't as exciting for them as defying a moderately tame response from our government, whose secret police probably won't disappear them, but it is an urgent requirement for the economically deprived in a time of a staggering economy. It would be laudable if the anti-war foes developed an ongoing constructive agenda that would supplement their voluble objections to United States policies, however questionable. Some of us appreciate that it's more fun to oppose things, until confronted by an impatient police officer who doesn't appreciate being insulted, spat upon and assaulted in violation of his/her rights.

While it is up to the people of Great Britain to request a reckoning from their government, it is up to Americans to demand an accounting from our government. The indignant protestors, by capturing headlines, allowed avaricious corporations latitude to move in to war-torn Iraq to feast on golden opportunities, without sufficient public scrutiny. It is neither reasonable nor just that select corporations will profit from the war, unless they helped pay for it. A further stipulation for corporations that want to profit from the war should be that the sons and daughters of their executives should have served in the military. Corporations should not get a free ride at the expense of the general public, who foot the bulk of our national bills. If corporations want to profit from liberating and rebuilding Iraq, let them share a significant portion of their profits by helping to rebuild our nation's deteriorating infrastructure. They could also contribute to our social services and educational systems that are staggering from budget shortfalls, yet face increasing needs of clients and students.

The whys of the war in Iraq will soon be the subject of historians. The moral questions will recede in the aftermath of victory and the responsibility for nation building. Yet the American people are entitled to a return from their investment in the war. It is an abuse of the public trust for certain corporations to profit from the peace, while millions of Americans do without food, medical services and the other critical requirements of the needy and underserved. The anti-war protestors, armored in righteousness, serve the status quo system by objecting to the horrible business of war and subsiding into indifference when the polarizing military actions cease to be dramatic enough. Yet the same outraged element abrogates any responsibility for the aftermath; the long, tedious, frustrating process of rebuilding a nation.

We, the people, paid for the war and we are entitled to be made aware of the guidelines under which corporations will be allowed to reap the plunder of war. The now falling silent vitriolic minority should help define the conditions under which corporations will be part of the rebuilding efforts. Any corporation that doesn't pay a just and equitable share of taxes should be automatically excluded from participation in any Iraq related contracts. Any corporation that set up offices abroad to evade domestic taxes should also be excluded from participation in any government contracts. It is apparent that the majority of our citizens and legislators ruled for war. Now it is imperative that the economic rights of the underserved be protected. The citizen taxpayers who paid for the war are entitled to be repaid with funds that will be put into vital public services. The economically deprived should be assisted with more funding for nutrition and health programs. New job development initiatives for the unemployed and those relegated to non-productive service jobs should be urgently addressed.

We have great domestic problems that desperately require intelligent solutions. We do not yet know how our economy and our society will thrive without an industrial manufacturing base, which is rapidly disappearing. The blue collar working class that was once considered the backbone of our country is evaporating. We must prepare for a future in which capital, corporations and jobs continue to leave the country. The enervating brain drain that goes abroad and the dumbing down of our culture at home, imperils the future of our country. It is convenient to protest our role in the world, especially when our actions are violent and brutal. However, in the ongoing age of volatile nation-states, war is condition normal, despite the horror it elicits in any sane human being. We need an equally dynamic anti-social and economic abuses movement, that will not burn out after several days of enjoyable street agitation.

Our nation requires a long term plan to regenerate the productive fabric of our society. Right now, the future well-being of the United States is completely dependent on the successful transformation of our economy from the predictable patterns of the Industrial era, to the speculative possibilities of the Information Age. How will we maintain the technical skills of the past while transacting data, instead of making or repairing things? It is obvious that new ideas are mandatory. Perhaps a condominium of government, universities, management and labor can forge a partnership in select industries that will ensure a future manufacturing capacity in defense, energy, communications, transportation, etc. Above all, government, the educational system, think tanks and not for profit organizations must prepare the public to recognize that it is necessary to formulate a long term plan for peace, as far down the road as it is for war.

Painting Reflects Theater

Commedia Del 'arte was the first professional form of theater and the forerunner of circus. From the renaissance to the Impressionists, art first reflected the spiritual, than the human condition. Painters from Callot through Watteau and Fragonard, up to Daumier, used Commedia as a commentary on the social conditions of their times. Commedia often presented an alternative to the artist's usual presentation of more formal subject matter. Beginning with Degas, there was a propensity by painters to stylize the Commedia actor as a clown figure. This obscured the range of skills, from ballet to drama, that Commedia once required of its actors as the first vehicle of professional performance. The neo-Impressionists, Fauves and Nabis, particularly Seurat, but including Signac, Bonnard, Vuillard, Matisse and Vlaminck, introduced the symbolic pathos of the clown and fool, as the alter-ego of the artist. Cezanne stabilized the conception of the actor as a type, establishing the image as a valid subject.

The movements that were truly responsive to the new technology of the 20th century; Cubism, Futurism, Dada, The Precisionists and Surrealism, presented the vitality of the actor, as well as the alienation of the artist from the life around him. Roualt, Picasso, Braque, Severini, Klee, Chagall, Calder and Miro, all explored the diverse relationships in the outcast mini-society of Le Cirque. The painters perceived Le Cirque as a lively, extroverted spectacle, surrounded by a hostile world, very much like the artist's.

The depiction of the color, humor, vulgarity, excitement, suffering and earthy vigor of Commedia brought identification, and admiration to many struggling artists. A revealing article by Theodore Riff, 'Harlequins, Saltimbanques, Clowns and Fools', illustrated the perception of so many modern artists, particularly Picasso, that led to the creation of many paintings. The expression of Roualt's torturous visions alternated between christ and the clown, indicating the conflict between the spirit and temptations of the flesh that tormented him.. Yet both spirit and flesh to the artist are frequently an anguish. Miro and Calder were among the few who expressed fun and joy in the subject of circus. Their use of childlike device returned the image of Commedia to one of its renaissance forms, vulgar comedy. Yet that is only a partial recognition of the historical influence of Commedia.

The wandering Commedia Del 'Arte troupes of the pre-Renaissance were generally the only entertainment, except for passion plays and jugglers, ever seen in the small towns of Italy, and later in France. The players presented the full range of performing arts, opera, ballet, classical drama and mannerist like comedy to the nobility, who paid a fee. Low comedy was primarily reserved for the lower classes. If the actors performed well for the peasants and merchants, and did not offend the audience with crude ad libs and insults at someone's expense, they were rewarded. They literally had to sing for their supper. If they got too familiar they might be beaten. By the time of the High Renaissance, the Commedia troupes had become professional touring companies, sponsored by kings and wealthy nobles. It was a fact of life then, as it still is now, that performing arts companies require generous patrons.

It is unclear how the myth began, that a Commedia actor played one character for his or her entire life. The cycle of aging from youth to elder manifestly demonstrates the fallacy of only playing one role. When actors were too old to be young lovers, swordfighters, acrobats, dancers, etc, they evolved to more mature roles; the jealous old man, the foolish doctor, the nurse, etc, as would as any skilled actor who develops his or her craft. Painters seem to have found the comedic element more appealing, perhaps as a diversion or assuagement from their own suffering. But the reality was that the actor was more than a 'fool', even though that's the image most presented by the painter.

The Republic of Dreams

The future of the American republic was frequently sustained by the timely appearance of notable leaders, who faced difficult issues that threatened the security and stability of the nation. Great presidents rose to the challenges that menaced the country, serving the people with desperately needed abilities. After their tenure, scholars and populist historians interpreted the significant events that led to wars, foreign interventions, or domestic crises, from the perspective of intellectual detachment, academic security and too often, indifference to the passions, doubts and confusions that shaped decision-making. Coincidental to the rise of globalism, with its traumatic impact on the American economy, may be the decline in the quality of our leadership, which is most tested in periods of extreme turmoil.

From pre-colonial times through World War II, the wars of America involved most of the citizenry, whether in combat, concern for loved ones, production of equipment and supplies, fund raising, civil defense, or countless other contributions to the war effort. Those who lost loved ones were pitied and respected, even by opponents of the war. And each war had its dissenters. Those who resisted the summons to arms out of high principle and protested the use of force from moral certitude, strengthened the fiber of the nation, since democracy requires the questioning of purpose, as long as it does not inhibit the need for necessary action for the survival of the nation.

Starting with Herodotus, recorded history reveals the perilous state of existence for nations and peoples, whose fate has invariably been decided by war. The clash of civilizations was inevitably resolved in battle. Empires were rarely dismantled peacefully and were traditionally dismembered by violence. The expansion of any nation was characterized by encroachment on another nation. Helpless peoples became slaves, or victims of exploitation. Pacifism was a condition of weakness, rather than moral virtue.

Everything changed in America after World War II. We righteously defeated totalitarianism and were ready to receive the fruits of victory; education, prosperity, the good life only previously envisioned by philosophers. But the world had contracted, due to a vast global confrontation that left fortress America vulnerably exposed to unprecedented threats. A terrible new enemy emerged, communism, potentially even more dangerous and menacing than fascism, with an ideology that had attracted many liberal westerners in the 1930's, who were dissatisfied with the shortcomings of democracy.

The United Nations, formed with the same high ideals as the League of Nations, became the public forum for two opposing blocs, as well as third world, supposedly unaligned, nations. Although World War III seemed inevitable, large stocks of nuclear weapons assured mutual destruction and tenuous accommodations were reached with the adversary. The greatest accomplishment of the twentieth century was the absence of a nuclear exchange between America and the Soviet Union. Wars of necessity became limited and the triumph of American arms was a relic of the past. People's wars of liberation, despite mostly being communist inspired, appealed to liberal intellectuals, who perceived a righteous cause and shut their eyes to mass liquidations and Gulags. At the same time, when America committed abuses, we were automatically judged guilty and condemned, because the world in general, and our citizens in particular, insisted we should behave better than others.

For various reasons spanning the gamut from egotism to ignorance, the liberal media, northeast intelligentsia and Hollywood leftists concluded that America was an aggressive oppressor, manipulated by an exploitative oligarchy for the benefit of a privileged few. Our policies were depicted as the major destructive force on the world stage. Whether these vociferous groups were correct in their sweeping judgments, or paranoid victims of delusion, is immaterial. Americans who accuse America of evil, do so from the bulwark provided by the security of democracy, a fundamental American institution. They demand a level of morality far more rigorous than applied to other nations, and refuse to recognize the need for real politik in a ferocious world. This arbitrary double standard may have birthed a great confusion in our youth.

However simplistic it may have been perceived by hyper-critical intellectuals, young Americans once aspired to the principles of a nation that were characterized by patriotism, loyalty and service. The Korean War, never explicated in a meaningful way to the public, left most of the country unaffected by the death of our men far away, except for those families who lost loved ones. There was no higher call to duty, no noble cause, no clear goals, only the defense of half an Asian people far away, from the other half of their countrymen, arbitrarily divided by cold war circumstances that made it normal to cut countries in half, to appease conflicting blocs. The intervention of communist China in Korea barely disturbed a nation already detaching itself from concern with the well-being of its military.

The Korean War ended in a stalemate, just about where it began, after the loss of thousands of American lives, with no clear result and for the first time in our wars, no victory. As the tensions of the cold war increased in the late 1950's, the dread of nuclear conflict permeated the American psyche. This created a schizoid personality in many young people, who were threatened by possible annihilation that they knew they were powerless to prevent, while at the same time they were encouraged to lead "normal" lives. Despite our nation's material prosperity, inconceivable in ages past, there was an unease underlying our way of life, a constant of the atomic age, that made us more stressed than previous generations.

The children who came of age in the 'sixties' were more dramatically divided into haves and have-nots than ever before. The haves, although amply provided with higher education and economic security, were not encouraged to develop traditional values by their parents, who were too absorbed in the pursuit of hitherto unattainable luxuries. Many young men from the blue collar class joined the military out of patriotism, opportunities for education, or even economic advancement. Regardless of their motivation, they served their country. Have-nots from the poverty communities were mostly drafted or joined to escape the harsh streets. Too many of the children of privilege evaded the draft, because they no longer esteemed our military and disdained military service.

The civil rights movement of the early sixties particularly stirred our college youth with a clear cut call to action in the struggle for equality. Moral virtue could hardly be disputed when it was opposed by hatred and discrimination. Then the Movement wound down and was replaced by the war in Vietnam as the national challenge. The youngsters who had felt empowered in a righteous cause, then thoughtlessly applied the same simple principles of right and wrong to a highly complex political and military conflict that was an integral facet of the Cold War.

In an irresponsible process of neglect, or deliberate mis-instruction, the best educated generation of young people in our history were left virtually ignorant of our appalling dependence on oil, the vast scope of the Cold War, the consequences of displaying weakness on the world stage and the historic fragility of the existence of democracy. Many young people felt that war was evil, and under the influence of sincere pacifists, fervent poets, hysteric entertainers, and raucous attention getters, they decided that America was evil, because of our assault on a distant peasant nation that imposed no threat to our well-being.

So while have-nots were fighting, bleeding and dying in remote Asian jungles and rice paddies, the haves were vigorously protesting our brutalities in our cities and campuses, until it was time to go home, or resume classes, or seek whatever diversion or entertainment appealed to them. The youth in combat had no choices. When the portable tv camera brought the Vietnam War, live and in color, into the living rooms and dorms of America, it made the horrors of war even more unpalatable to inexperienced youth. At the same time, the cameras, live and in color, brought anti-war demonstrations into living rooms, dorms, G.I. barracks and foreign countries, presenting a pageant of venomous dissent that hadn't been seen in America since the Civil War. Rabid opposition to 'Lyndon's War' actually ended his presidency.

When the Vietnam War finally concluded in our ignominious defeat, many Americans gloated at our discomfiture, further alienating an already bitter military, who felt they had been forsaken by the nation, while they were fighting far away. At the same time, our universities, erstwhile providers of knowledge, seemed to be more concerned with the accumulation of real estate and amassing of assets. Instead of requiring courses in the harsh realities of the world, and more math and science to continue our technology, they offered more fine arts. They did not inform gullible students that the sword decides the fate of nations more often than the pen. It was another sign that our society was becoming too comfortable to struggle against the vicissitudes of life, except part-time. The lessons of natural tragedies; earthquakes, hurricanes, floods, disease, as well as man-made disasters; war, train crashes, auto accidents, hand gun violence, occurrences that should remind us that life is fragile, perilous, fraught with risk, were softened for too many of us by the protective cocoon of amenities.

After the fall of Saigon in 1975, America retreated into its shell for the rest of the decade, opting for diplomacy and trade, in preference to military adventure. The Reagan administration advocated a strong military and resistance to the 'Evil Empire' of the Soviet Union that confronted us globally. This challenge of the 'eighties' saw the resurgence of the struggle between the 'hawks' and the 'doves'. President Reagan's urgency for the Strategic Defense Initiative, 'Star Wars', provoked opposition from the same type of anti-war groups that had protested in the 'sixties', without their previous vigor and clarity of purpose. The scientific complexities of 'Star Wars' precluded the involvement of most actors and poets, who were ill-equipped to dispute the issues. Since 'Star Wars' was mostly research, few instances for volatile confrontation and insufficient publicity discouraged many attention-seeking radicals from active protest.

The collapse of the Soviet Union ended a competition that fortuitously never erupted in horrendous nuclear war. Proxy wars had replaced direct conflict and the culture of war in America was in disrepute. Any consideration of military options was instantly opposed by anti-war elements, regardless of circumstances. This vocal resistance was echoed by several allies in NATO, no longer dependant on the United States for protection from the big, bad Russian bear. While our economy boomed in the 'nineties' and enriched the world, resentment for our power and culture became condition normal, especially in the Moslem world. Somehow, despite helping the world more than any country in history, we were losing our friends and making new enemies. At the same time, the nation that was founded on continuous conflict had lost its appetite for war.

Although we forged a broad alliance in the first Gulf War and achieved the first notable military victory in two generations, the situation of America did not change significantly for the better. In fact, the rise of the Euro-Union fostered an economic rivalry between two great industrialized blocs that created growing differences between them. Conflicts of interest, suppressed during the apprehensions of the Cold War, surfaced with increasing regularity. All the doubts that had distressed America in the 'sixties', reemerged as our economy spiraled down and we couldn't seem to do anything right on the world stage. Businesses were taking their capital abroad. Jobs were being outsourced, especially high paying industrial and technical positions, leaving bleaker opportunities for discontented workers in lower paying security and service jobs.

The dot.com collapse assailed an economy struggling with massive trade deficits, disappearing industries and growing apprehensions that

America's time in the sun was winding down. Public confidence in our leaders was stretched thin and media second- guessing of every event further extended the plagues of doubt and confusion. Politics had virtually become ossified in a two party system. In the 2000 election, democrats actually blamed a third party candidate for the loss of the presidency for their party. Slightly reminiscent of the decadence of ancient Rome, when 'Blues' and 'Greens' struggled for power, the two major parties frowned on alternatives, abrogating the people's right to a candidate of their choice.

9/11 changed the emotional landscape of America, presenting us with a moral crusade against terror. Among other results, this distracted us from difficult or unsolveable problems that would not go away, but were suddenly less threatening. However distressed we might be by diminishing incomes and fewer opportunities, the menace of terror became our overwhelming priority. Domestic security was suddenly so important that it eclipsed other vital concerns for the long term future. Our scientific and technical lead over the rest of the world was rapidly evaporating. More than half of the ph.d candidates in our graduate school programs are foreigners, studying math, physics and other sciences. They will return to their countries and help advance development. Many of our ph.d candidates are in the arts, soft sciences and physical education. The disparity for the future is alarming.

We cannot suppose that our nation is at crossroads. That would presume clear choices. We may be facing the most perilous time in the history of the republic. A time of industrial, technical, scientific, perhaps even moral decline, that leaves our vulnerable citizens apprehensive, our aware citizens uneasy. Our ailing system indicates that we cannot resurrect obsolete industries and compete in the world market in manufacturing products that are produced cheaper and better abroad. It has not been determined if our advanced technical industries can sustain a nation. The gulf between haves and have-nots keeps widening to the point of creating a de facto oligarchy. It is uncertain if the wounded giant can regenerate itself. We urgently need great leadership to steer us through these ominous pitfalls. New directions and new horizons must be found, before the republic of dreams dwindles to a second world reality.

The American Burden

The status of illegal aliens in America is now being likened to immigrants past, welcomed to our beneficent shores for the search of life, liberty and the pursuit of.... But millions of recent arrivistes determined to undermine the principal of sovereignty, first established by the Treaty of Westphalia in 1648, scorn our right of refusal. This uninvited population has garnered the usual support from vested business interests, churches eager to refill empty pews, politicians hungering to retain or attain office, the liberal media and left-wing extremists eager for any cause that opposes the American government. The nation-wide demonstrations for the rights of immigrants are attempting to obfuscate the real issue. Illegal aliens aren't immigrants. They entered the country illegally. They are not entitled to any American rights, simply because they should not be here. If they have elected to bypass the normal procedures of immigration, we are under no obligation to them.

Recent estimates suggest that there may be eleven to twelve million illegal aliens in the United States. If we subtract the unknown number of undesirables, gang members, dopers, smugglers, perverts, criminals of various persuasions and possible terrorists, we are left with millions of undocumented people with minimal to no commitments to the United States. Not only do they have a limited inclination to learn English, once a precursor to citizenship, they even want to sing our national anthem in a foreign language. Even if we erect impenetrable barriers around fortress America to restrict illicit access to our diminishing opportunities, we are still left with a large segment of unwanted intruders who are eager to participate in our benefits, but reluctant to share our burdens.

The examples of the civil rights movement, the anti-Vietnam war movement and the gay rights movement will be emulated by the emerging immigrant rights movement, until they achieve the goal of unrestricted entry to the bountiful United States. In order to maintain national sovereignty and to preserve the right to determine who is welcome on our shores, it is necessary to assert control over our borders. All illegal aliens must be identified and documented before their righteous and religious advocates arbitrarily transmute them into legitimate immigrants, just because they are here.

Since it is too late to mandate transit through Ellis Island, or equivalent points of entry for those already here, it is increasingly urgent to apprehend and treat appropriately all illegal aliens, before we are compelled to accept them by force of media clamor, pandering politicians and high-priced public relations firms. The first step to resolution of this crisis will be to isolate the alien population by issuing every legal citizen a temporary, hi-tech I.D card. Sensors that read the cards will be temporarily installed in all workplaces, shopping centers, schools, highways, parks, playgrounds, hospitals and public gathering places, until the crisis is resolved.

A security force of alien identification monitors (AIM) will be recruited to staff all sensor installations. Another unit will be developed to apprehend and detain anyone undocumented, or carrying false documentation. All detainees will be taken to temporary processing centers in underutilized public buildings, or in other temporary holding facilities. A special corps of lawyers and judges will be appointed to review each person's case. All able-bodied men and women without criminal or other disqualifying records will be offered the opportunity to enlist in a public service corps, as a prerequisite for citizenship. They will then attend an educational and training curriculum which will prepare them for public service. Eligible men and women will be offered the opportunity to enlist in the armed forces of the United States to earn citizenship.

The vast majority of the detainees will be unwilling or unqualified to do service as a means to achieve citizenship. Since it is economically unfeasible to apprehend, detain, then deport millions of unacceptable aliens, we will create an emergency prison system, with individual institutions to be located in depressed communities that will gain the benefits of jobs, support services and cash flow characteristic of the growth phenomena of the domestic prison industry. Motivational and educational training will prepare the incarcerated population for either some form of public service, or they will endure long term detention.

Funding will be provided by an act of congress increasing the national debt by two hundred and fifty billion dollars. An already burdensomely mortgaged society will readily invest in a future that will conduce to more domestic tranquility, the removal of unfair competition for low-paying jobs and give many beleaguered Americans the patriotic satisfaction of reestablishing the rule of law and order in a socially challenged nation. The future mandates drastic action for a massive problem, lest our grandchildren be packed shoulder to shoulder with millions and millions of undesirable neighbors, wantonly consuming our limited resources.

The Perils of Decline

In the Hegalian tradition of philosophy there is a concept relative to the rise and fall of civilization. Purely for the sake of reason we are interested in Hegal's "antithesis", which would be the temporary decline of a culture preceding a glorious renaissance. We shall use the example of the waning culture of America to question the wisdom of Hegal, and express the fear that even a dedicated and capable leadership, which we have been deprived of for lo these many years, could not salvage a once promising techno-industrial empire, bankrupted and beggared by its own greedy capitalist exploiters

Looking back at the childhood of George W. Bush, no one could imagine that he was destined in later years to hold the highest office in the venerable government, once the envy of the world, now the most hated. Despite the accomplishments of his father, George Bush, Senior, who after holding various important government positions was elected to the highest office, Junior's beginnings were undistinguished. He was at best of average intelligence, a distressing condition for a chief executive in a society already afflicted with Dumbing Down Syndrome, (DDS).

Junior's educational career was mediocre, characterized by barely passing grades in college and participation in alcohol and drug consumption, a frequent activity of many young Americans of privilege, who were completely oblivious to their responsibilities to their nation and the future. Unlike the clever Clinton, who followed Bush, Senior, Junior performed military service, all-be-it removed from any war zone. But he became a jet fighter pilot, thereby at least partially refuting the suspicions of his being an early victim of DDS.

In what many Americans believed to be a veritable, although minor miracle, Junior was transformed and became a local government leader, exhibiting confidence and sincerity. Then, in what many considered an even greater miracle, despite the disputed results, he was elected to the highest office in the land. His oligarch manipulators, interested only in profits from investments and their continued well-being, were unconcerned with the collapse of American industry, the decay of public institutions and a crushing national debt that condemned future Americans to poverty and deprivation. But the oligarchs needed to divert the people while they milked the system for the last bit of gain, regardless of the harm done to the nation.

Therefore, according to tried and true American tradition whenever the way of life of the privileged was threatened, they resorted to a time honored solution; the declaration of an appropriate foreign war. This would be presented to the public as a democratic crusade against a particularly distasteful group of foreigners who threatened the stability of the world order, menaced their neighbors, practiced ethnic cleansing, harbored terrorists, or in the bestest ever justification for military action, were seeking weapons of mass destruction.

In an age where the media are owned by those who do not have the best interests of the people as their prime motive, access to information regarding critical decision-making by the general public is extremely limited. In fact, Americans have been allowed until recently to accumulate so much in the way of goods and services, that except when it affects them personally, many tend to accept information from the media at face value and ignore questionable activities of their government. The internet, once heralded as a democratizing institution, is merely another manifestation of circus, to divert the people from vital issues.

When a president with the power to virtually incinerate the world becomes righteous about issues that are conceived to disguise rapacious economic imperialism, promulgated by military force, a hopeful society is betrayed and precipitated to an undesirable future. In a world still dominated by nationalism, of course America, as a vaunted hegemon, is the recipient of unmitigated suspicion and hatred. Americans, persuaded by their leaders and the media that they are supporting a just cause, are as much victims as their government's targets of external aggression. A people once promised a better life than their parents were abandoned by the oligarchs, with the tacit consent of their elected officials, as far back as the 'sixties', when capital was moved to investments abroad, leaving us the inheritance of the rust belt and other depressed areas that blight the nation. The fallout of industrial collapse polluted everyone but the capitalists who pioneered outsourcing. Today outsourcing is blamed for loss of jobs, but it started long ago.

The president is an excellent figurehead to receive our criticisms and grievances, but he is merely a tool of ruthless, amoral manipulators, whose only concern is for their accumulation and maintenance of money and power. Many of the social and economic evils in America are the products of the selfishness of private interests, who yearn for a third yacht, while American children are malnourished. These acts are abusive, as well as exploitive. However, who can we trust to lead us to a better world? France? Russia? Egypt? China? Is there a nation less guilty than America of international violations of the law? Is it possible that better the government we have, than one we know not of? As Iran sinks backwards to the middle ages, except in the development of modern armaments, how will America endure the threats that confront it?

Contemporary historians, especially the glib and clever one's, who are sheltered in their secure fortresses of academia and do not have to struggle for their daily bread, are quick to condemn our president and America for their crimes against humanity. However, these vociferous critics have nothing better to offer and only add to the leaks in the lifeboats of survival. As we submerge under the burden of industrial decay, whether in gradual decline, or rapid collapse, the most obvious diagnosis of our civic body reveals a total lack of wisdom that can be used for problem solving, domestic or foreign. The future of our society is grim without meaningful answers for critical needs that will enable our children to endure uncertain tomorrows.

The Antigone Syndrome

A princess of the great house of Laius, that rules Thebes, has everything her world provides. Her parents, Oedipus and Jocasta, rule wisely and well. She is betrothed to Haemon, son of Creon, brother of Jocasta, the foremost lord in the land, after the king and princes, Eteocles and Polyneices.

Antigone has wealth, luxury, position and love, until plague strikes Thebes. Oedipus sends for Tiresias, the blind prophet, who reluctantly reveals the plague is punishment for Oedipus' patricide and incest. Jocasta hangs herself in shame. Oedipus blinds himself and renounces the throne.

Eteocles and Polyneices, one of whom will be king, do not seem to be overly distressed at the revelation that their father is their brother and their mother is their sister. They are powerful lords, to be feared if provoked by public comment. They agree to alternate rulership and Eteocles rules first.

Antigone and her fragile sister, Ismene, must live with the shame and humiliation of being offspring of incestuous parents. When they venture out of the palace, they feel the oppression of judgment by the people of the city, who do not dare confront them openly. The shame is unbearable, yet they must persevere, determined by their class and position. But Thebes is a small kingdom and everyone knows their dreadful story and awaits further disaster, which they believe will inevitably strike this cursed House.

At the end of Eteocles agreed term of rulership, he refuses to vacate the throne. He banishes Polyneices, who returns with an army and besieges Thebes. The long suffering Thebans had endured the Sphinx killing anyone who entered or left the city, who couldn't answer the riddle: what walks on four legs in the morning, two legs in the afternoon and three legs in the evening? Oedipus' answer, man, vanquished the Sphinx and freed the city. Then Thebes was ravaged by plague. Now war was devouring their children and loved ones in the struggle between two brothers for rulership.

Antigone and Ismene were surely blamed for the woes inflicting the people, for it was the curse on their House that brought these horrors to Thebes.

When Eteocles and Polyneices fought in single combat and killed each other, Creon, brother of Jocasta, became king. He proclaimed honorable burial rites for Eteocles, who defended his city, but exposure to the wild beasts for Polyneices, who attacked his city.

Antigone went to Creon, surely a demeaning action for a former great princess to beg of her uncle, and asked permission to give burial rites to her brother, according to law and custom. Creon refused. She insisted it was her duty to give her brother burial rights, desperate to overcome her shame by performing the honorable ritual.

Creon issued a proclamation: 'Anyone giving burial rites to Polyneices would be killed'. Antigone left defiantly, asserting it was her duty to the gods to give her brother burial rites. Creon's son, Haemon, knowing how stubborn they both were, tried to intervene to save his betrothed, but Creon wouldn't listen.

Antigone, driven to near madness by shame, gave Polyneices burial rites, perhaps seeking redemption in the hallowed ritual. Creon found out and had her buried alive. Haemon killed himself and Ismene went mad, thus tragically ending the rule of the House of Laius.

Antigone, a woman of intelligence, beauty. breeding, had everything, then lost everything to cruel fate, which destroyed her for the sins of her father's father. She was an innocent victim, who might have become a great queen, but became a tragic figure, a creature to be pitied, possibly admired by a few, for her death with honor. Yet it is reasonable to assume that Antigone could not live with the burden fate had placed on her and chose to die, rather then live with shame.

The actress must create a complex role, but perform it simply, so the audience feels her anguish and pities her for her loss and suffering. Yet this is not a dramatic reenactment, nor the scholarly retelling of a myth. This is a passionate, soaring character, tormented by the horrible discovery of her parents relationship and her brothers' death. She is noble, dignified, arrogant, righteous, tortured and prefers death to a life of shame. The actress must make the audience feel her character's suffering, in order to sustain the intensity of the play.

Emergency Alert

The mushrooming incidents of deranged violence threaten the future security of American society and must be addressed urgently, if we hope to preserve any semblance of domestic stability. Three more frequently occurring types of clinically insane behavior that must be defended against are: 1) homicidal assaults on our schools; 2) horrific abductions, torture and murder of young girls; 3) spurned husbands, fiancées, or boyfriends murdering the women who rejected them. There are many other criminal aberrations that erode the fabric of our culture, but the three examples are related for their unique, long-term debilitating effects on our citizenry.

When juvenile students go on a shooting spree in their schools to avenge grievances, real or imagined, they are telling us that the system failed them, and consequently, their teachers and peers. There appears to be a developing occurrence of fellow students alerting the authorities to potential attacks, which is laudable. However, that is insufficient to insure deterrence and does not address the cause. The loss of life in an incident and the traumatic consequences of the aftermath, warrant vital prevention programs to avert tragic events. Prevention is economically cheaper than the cost of disasters with their resultant loss and emotional trauma, and should be among the highest priorities considered by the educational system.

A rampaging loner, later characterized by friends and family as 'a nice, quiet person who they couldn't imagine doing that', who storms a school, terrifies, then executes his captives, is among a nation's worst nightmares. Recent events have demonstrated that this can happen in any community, small or large. While post-mortems and conferences take place, there is an urgent need to take action before the spread of the virus that will produce copycats. Every school in America that does not have entrance security must recruit retired senior citizen volunteers, preferably ex-military or law enforcement, who will become guardians of the vulnerable portals that shelter our children, until another, long-term solution is achieved.

A nation's youth is its most precious commodity, although self-serving oligarchs who can afford security for their offspring may disagree. Our schools are the construction sites of our future, despite the neglect of science for indulgence in the liberal arts. It is preferable that we not turn our learning institutions into armed fortresses under siege. Yet we must protect our youth from demented attack in what should be the safety of their educational environments. This is a vital national issue because it transcends state boundaries and, as we have recently seen, can erupt anywhere. Therefore we must recognize these acts as domestic terrorism, which require urgent preventive measures.

Conspiracy theorists cite these events as another motivational pressure to further isolate the individual, who is already withdrawing into the cocoon of the internet, use of which is invariably a solitary activity practiced at home. Whether their suppositions are fantasy, foolishness, or fact, one condition of human life is self-evident. It is a cooperative venture. If everyone, in a traditional science fiction scenario, is ensconced in the automated isolation of home, the community of our society will be terminated. The conclusion is obvious. We must protect our schools and better nurture and educate our students.

The abduction of children who are sexually abused, tortured, then murdered is a primal violation of the child, the family and the society. Our young, unlike most in nature, are not born capable of soon looking out for themselves. We have devised innumerable conventions to nurture slow developers. Fundamental, however, must always be the first law, physical protection from harm. When twisted individuals abduct a child in the most heinous of crimes, it destroys the innocent victim, shatters the family and dissolves a society's belief in the aegis of law and morality.

If human nature has once again reached the stage of <u>homo hominis lupus</u>, drastic measures are called for to stem the rising evil tide of aberration. It may be far fetched to suggest that these terrible crimes are by-products of a failed state and occur as Noam Chomsky asserts, when: "it becomes necessary to divert and control the public in some fashion". However. Is it beyond the realm of possibility that the privileged elite who permit millions of Americans to go hungry while they feast on ever-diminishing resources, allow these dreadful events? Are the only options to securing the safety of our children tolerating a police state, or home isolation? We must develop a system to identify and locate individuals who are a direct threat to our vulnerable youth, then correct, incarcerate or execute them, before they murder our innocents.

In another form of the virulent disease that attacks our schools and children we have a growing plague of rejectionism backlash. With increasing frequency, a woman is not being allowed to reject her suitor. This is not merely a violation of the individual's rights, it is another assault on the customs, mores and mating rituals of our society. If a woman does not dare say no, she will either accept the intolerable burden of oppression and pass it on to others by exposure, or reject dating, courtship, or mating out of fear of violence. The consequences of either situation are fraught with negatives and further fray the fabric of a society that still aspires to prevent chaos and lawlessness.

Whether we are entering a period of human nature gone astray, or we are under assault by manipulative forces. We must find a cure for the developing cancers of insane violence that will otherwise destroy our public confidence and erode the trust in the day to day functioning of our society. Intrusions into individual and collective civil rights are always to be regarded with fear and suspicion. Yet the intrusive assaults on our way of life must be prevented, if we are to retain any semblance of public order and stability. Short term security can be improved by increased implementation of standard procedures and volunteerism. Longer term solutions require innovative changes. One possible option is to create a crime prevention academy, on the lines of the military service academys, inculcating the highest levels of training in the skills of law enforcement, science and morality in dedicated public servants. The warning is clear. We are required to take action or further abet our evolutionary descent.

Social Speculation

The future of American society is intolerably tainted by the pernicious effects of television. This is not merely the medium that emits torrential commands to millions of hypnotized viewers to buy some kind of product, glamorously presented to convince us of its appeal. Tv includes programming of extreme violent and sexual content that assaults the concept of morality and inures us until we accept anti-social behavior. It is a vehicle that seduces the public, evolving us to a sedentary mass that will result in our no longer being capable of determining right from wrong. There is also a more destructive aspect to this mindwash. The standard home situation, where our precious sons or daughters, faces fixated upon the television set, our refuge, our curse, are optically denuded and suborned of their potential to acquire the learning initiative, is now a cultural norm. In an era of dynamic progress, capable youth will be critically needed in the future if we hope to maintain a functional society.

Today our science propels our existence with accessible technology, producing incredible innovations. Those thinkers among us who point out that we are years behind ourselves morally, frequently go unheeded. The radical right has usurped the custody of morality and seeks to impose a restrictive code of behavior on the nation. The devious minds who offer the theory of 'Intelligent Design' as a slicker packaging of Creationism, are attempting to turn back the clock to an earlier age of scientific repression. This disparity should lead us to impose a question: who is determining the fate of our society? The gross misuse of power in the hands of irresponsible leaders is analogous to placing a number of children, with very sharp knives, in a small crowded room, from which the adults depart with the concerned admonition: "Don't hurt yourselves."

If the human race is to survive the coming calamities that we have engineered; global warming, depletion of the ozone layer, deforestation, disasters man-made, as well as those imposed by nature, we require a new kind of leadership and new directions in national policy. In a world wracked with poverty, disease, hunger, ethnic hatreds and endless wars, we need wise and skilled guardians, who could try to salvage our planet, before it is too late. The highest priority of the United Nations and all functional first world governments, should be to locate and nurture a new class of leaders, techno-humanists, who might possibly construct the only potential direction for earthly survival. An international academy should be created, recruiting potential candidates worldwide, for service dedicated to civilization's continuation. An independent commission under U.N. auspices would screen applicants for the required technical, conceptual and moral skills mandatory for world guidance. After sufficient preparation, their task would be to reeducate humanity in how to preserve our planet. (Academy curricula and operations plan available on request by designated representatives of heads of state and the U.N.)

Protest Oui, Alternative Non

There are no valid comparisons between the anti-war movement during the Vietnam war and the developing protests against war with Iraq, except for possible anti-American sentiment. One fundamental difference is that the Vietnam protests evolved gradually, after the war became a major American military intervention. The protesters against war with Iraq are attempting to prevent war, regardless of the issues that cause America to threaten war. During the Vietnam war there was no menace from weapons of mass destruction, or threat of attacks on the homeland. The problem today is that apart from some of our citizens' objections to American unilateralism, there is an unanswered question of who will police the world, if the United Nations does not take action.

Except for activists like Reverend Muste, the Berrigans and Mitchell Goodman, very few of the Vietnam war protestors understood the nature of the cold war confrontation. They certainly did not recognize the U.S. involvement in Vietnam until the mid-sixties, many years after the escalation of our military presence. Even fewer of the anti-war foes had any conception of great power politics and the concomitant realities of dealing with state sponsored aggression in a seething, nationalistic world. They were oblivious to the hatreds, fears and envy of certain demonstrators who were opponents of American power and who exploited the anti-war movement for their own ends. Not many protestors came from the have-nots, unlike the civil rights movement, which spanned the entire spectrum of our society and allowed us a simple moral choice, for or against.

One of the key elements of the Vietnam protest that is insufficiently discussed is that dissenters had only one agenda, end the war. They weren't concerned with the dangers of the cold war struggle. They were conflicted about the capitalist economy that was gobbling up as much of the world as it could devour, yet that produced luxuries and comforts for the very people who were opposing the system. For the most part, the protest leaders had no solutions to the vast array of complex problems that challenged America. Nor were they concerned with solutions to the economic, political and military problems that confronted us. Instead, they manipulated the media in their willingness to break down the fabric of our society as they opposed the war, without facing the issues that caused the war.

Only profiteers, the ambitious, or lunatics want war. Every reasonable human being should know that war is the most terrible event that mankind has devised. Yet until there is universal justice and regulation of aggression, war is a dreadful reality. We live in a world that has not yet evolved enough to create a reliable international body that can prevent or resolve most disputes. The United Nations is enormously more effective than the League of Nations ever was, but it is still restricted by the special interests of the membership and operates under severe limitations. Anti-war protestors don't realize that only an impartial international body with authority and power can regulate the conflicts of nations. In the absence of such a body, individual nations must act on their own behalf. The United States, in its military restraint and charitable concerns with the effects of war and its aftermath, is arguably more benevolent than other nations. Yet many protestors believe we are the only nation abusing its power.

With dozens of wars taking place in the world, it is a peculiar phenomenon to see American citizens protesting a possible war with Iraq, when they are seemingly unconcerned about ongoing wars elsewhere. Unlike notable protestors of the 'sixties', the most visible spokespersons against war with Iraq are Hollywood actors. Of course they are as entitled to their opinions, as are any other members of our society, but their limited background in foreign policy, history, economics, science, politics and military affairs makes it inappropriate for them to tell the American people what to do. Their level of political consciousness is far more suitable to internet chat rooms, than public forums. It is an indication of the intellectual poverty of our country that actors are the most prominent protestors on foreign policy. If we could only end war by objecting to it, what a great day it would be for the human race, but that is not reality.

In a world of violent leaders, abetted by compliant followers, armed, or aspiring to be armed with weapons of mass destruction, it is insufficient to just oppose war. We need practical solutions to the threats that abound from many nations, not simplistic anti-war rhetoric. Western democracies were confronted with the menace of fascism in the 'thirties' and did not respond until it was too late for many countries that were ravaged by aggression. The cold war, which occurred with the concomitant means of viewing ongoing events on television, may have been the most traumatic period in history. The global struggle between two opposing superpowers was presented daily to the public, provoking endless fears, without providing answers. Now that the cold war is over, America is the remaining military superpower, and may be the only nation determined enough to attempt to prevent the spread of weapons of mass destruction.

When Americans in the 'sixties' reviled their country and praised Ho Chi Minh, they at least selected a staturous adversary in Uncle Ho, who had won the acclaim of his people for a struggle against colonialism and who resisted the division of his country, the division of countries being a peculiar characteristic of the cold war. Saddam Hussein appears to have no admirers, save those who cherish brutal dictators. Those who oppose war with Iraq are invariably anti-war, no matter with whom, but they also seem to be anti-American foreign policy. In a constitutional democracy, some citizens nurtured on creature comforts and liberal arts educations may not sufficiently recognize the unfriendly intentions of other nations. We cannot in fairness criticize anyone who abhors war. However, in a perilous world rushing faster and faster to the deployment of weapons of mass destruction, we need more comprehensive directives than 'No war.'

If the anti-war with Iraq protestors are to serve the best interests of their world, they must also consider the best interests of their country. Let them propose alternate options to war. Let them present practical ways to resolve difficult confrontational situations with potentially dreadful consequences. Many of the anti-war protestors are too sheltered from the harsh realities of the world and blame America for its ills, while profiting from the benefits of the American way of life. Any hysteric can rant about the faults of our country. Any hopeful flower child can urge us to 'make love, not war.' Concerned people who oppose war should also accept the responsibility of finding practical solutions to the problems that lead to war.

The Decline of Drama

The future of serious drama in America is in imminent danger of eclipse, since it is failing to develop new audiences to replace the rapidly diminishing base of aging attendees. The performing arts in general, opera, ballet, classical music, have always appealed to a culturally elite audience, but theater once reached many more levels of society. The evolving visual assault of cinema and tv has conditioned several generations to passive spectation. The requirement of emotional involvement in the life of a play has become alien to detached viewers, who are more accustomed to sitting back and observing passively. While the elite performing arts will continue to ebb away, theater may still be regenerated, if urgently needed dynamic changes are implemented.

A brief survey of the obstacles that threaten the preservation of serious drama in America is daunting. The diminishing audience of serious theater goers is not being replaced. More and more Off-Broadway houses are closing because of exorbitant costs that make production economically unviable. Broadway houses are presenting fewer and fewer classics and serious dramas, except for the spate of Irish playwrites. Since grade schools and high schools generally do not introduce students to serious drama, the competition of hi-tech video games and action films is erasing the opportunity for developing new theater audiences. Serious drama is submerging under the pressure of HDTV. The message of serious theater, the emotional and intellectual exploration of life, is being lost.

In order to reinvolve audiences in the excitement of theater, the education and training of the actor, the direct transmitter of theater, must be redefined to satisfy the need for intense involvement in the play. The development of the serious stage actor is virtually in conflict, technique-wise, with actors for television, commercials, movies and musicals. Colleges and universities have supplanted professional theater companies in training theater practitioners. They must recognize, then inform the students, that the dramatic stage actor has little chance of fame, fortune, even satisfactory work, yet should prepare with dance-like dedication to master the skills necessary to bring drama to life. The students must be made to understand that the dramatic stage actor is not better than other actors, just different.

Since academia has replaced the professional theater as the training ground for actors, it should be obvious that the standard curricula may be insufficient to properly develop the actor, since talented stage actors no longer thrill audiences. If the dramatic theater is to survive and contribute to the political, social and cultural life of our society, new methods of preparation must be explored. The student actors must be informed of the pitfalls of their choice. If they decide to continue, they should enter an ensemble-like training program that will develop the mental, emotional, vocal and physical skills that are mandatory to bring classics, social issue plays and other serious drama, in absorbing presentation, to audiences overly bombarded with entertainment and stimuli.

The other vital element of theater, the director, is also failing to produce theatrical thrills and chills. Student directors should be trained to understand the nature of the classics, invariably upper class documents, that lose vitality when casually transliterated into the spectrum of mafia dons and drug lords. They should be taught that the play is the concept, as well as the blueprint for production. Arbitrary updating merely reduces the scale of characters, from lofty to squalid. Concepts, as the au courant interpretation of drama, must be reexamined and revised for a more structured approach to theater. Granted, the era of the actor and the era of the playwrite have given way to the era of the director, nevertheless, the director may not be the ideal custodian of theater, unless he or she accepts the responsibility to preserve true theater values, currently a foreign conception.

The academic encouragement to develop a directorial concept to revitalize a play is misguided. The play must be the concept. If necessary, let the directors also become playwrites. That is a long, glorious tradition in the history of theater. Let the directors explore improvised works. Let them have license to create new forms, but educate them to the nature of responsibility to the play. It may not be their fault that audiences no longer seem to get very excited about drama, but they are certainly contributory. Directors must be educated to understand that the difference between a classic and new play is akin to the separation of church and state.

There is serious work for only a fraction of director graduates with degrees in fine arts, (as well as for actors). There must be a winnowing out of the candidates for a particular discipline of directing, concentrating on a specialty, combined with a general procedure of giving them a little bit of everything. A director who can't read music will not function well in musical theater. A director who can't utilize cameras is not meant for film or television. Drama departments must advise, then encourage the development of skills and knowledge necessary for the highest performance values in the production of theater. They need not rule out cross disciplines, but they should differentiate between the various forms of theater. A thorough knowledge of classical literature and appropriate period history is vital for exciting drama presentation. The Industrial Revolution, especially from the 1850's, should be understood as a major time of change from upper class drama to middle class drama. Process must be developed by directors and actors in order to construct the appropriate world of the play in its proper context; past, present, or future. The goal should be to prepare passionate productions that present the art of theater, not scholarly documents, museum artifacts, or dilettante indulgences.

One of the great contributions to the demise of serious theater is the showcase system. The idea of extremely limited rehearsal time that results in a few slapdash performances is contradictory to the nature of theater. The lack of commitment to the play by actors, who are encouraged by their union to leave at any time for paid work, undermines the tradition of theater. This concept of commercially inspired presentation of actors or directors, who shoddily display their wares to agents or producers, erodes the very foundation of theater. No other performing art would offer such ill-prepared, ill-disciplined and superficial presentations in the hope of peddling talent.

The aberration of the showcase system is just one of the many factors that have caused the current crisis in theater. One fact is clear. If we don't reach our audiences and make them come back to our theaters, the future of American drama will have been squandered by the present custodians. We should consider remembering that the reapplication of a traditional principle, the show must go on, might be an element that would help rebuild a fraying relationship between audience and practitioner. The theater world must act soon, or else it will go the way of all narrow-based performing arts.

The Danger of Dumbing Down

In a world grown progressively smaller due to faster air transportation and more rapid electronic transmission of information, there are increasing threats to American security from a spectrum of enemies. One of the most dangerous domestic problems is the growing intellectual incapacity of our youth. The multiplicity of challenges facing our nation, possibly reminiscent of the decline of the Roman Empire when it could no longer muster resources to meet all exigencies, mandates an urgent assessment of priorities to insure our survival and well-being. In the past, when wars occurred, often the combatants fought on after the governments made peace. Sometimes hostilities took years for resolution. Today the capacity and means for destruction is growing so sophisticated that soon a devastating war could be over before a nation could respond. In the event of cyberwar, a nation might conceivably not even know it was attacked.

There appear to be several distinctly different types of warfare that America will face in the future; protracted insurgency, terrorist delivery of weapons of mass destruction, limited pre-emption or intervention, or escalation into total war, a prospect horrible to imagine, but which must be considered. It is becoming evident that we lack the wherewithal to deal with all possible scenarios simultaneously, yet the possibility exists that multiple confrontations could present a calamitous reality. With insufficient means to deal with all problems, a triage procedure must be invoked to prioritize the appropriate responses to the most urgent problems. We must also better prepare our capacity for planning for future exigencies

The current world situation and the complexity of national issues requires a leadership that is wise, just, firm, expedient, as well as a host of other abilities vital to the decision making process. We sometimes get leaders who possess some of the necessary qualities for governance, but never enough to resolve long term crises. Wisdom seems to have abandoned us completely, perhaps eradicated among other causes by the numbing early exposure in our youth to the artificial values and deceptive nature of television. The constant flow of visual imagery that stipulates passive spectation, stifles the creative energies characteristic of developing youth and insures the channeling of their potential into limited directions

A nation of video game players may be preferable to a nation of sheep, but they will be incapable of addressing the vast scope of the problems of tomorrow. The educational system ignores the extreme capacity for learning inherent in youth. Instead of motivating the youngest attendees to expand their scope, followed by increased demands to absorb more and more, they are fed pablum, or left behind. The future of our society is being entrusted to students of the arts, rather than students of math and the sciences. Yet those who cannot meet the highest standards must nevertheless be respected and taught to appreciate their gifts, but only after sufficient effort to educate them. The only hope for the survival of the frayed American dream is to prepare our youth for the inevitable struggles to come.

If we allow the majority of our youngsters to dwindle in their ability to participate actively in the tending of our society, we permit the privileged few to dominate the affairs of state. Just because they lead by virtue of their material circumstances, does not mean they are suitable for the positions they achieve through self-serving networks. Those who achieve on their own merits often succumb to the corrupters, who take advantage of the ambitious. The nation is more important than it's constituent parts and requires service from its citizens. The dumbing down of our people, with sensory overload being a major factor, imperils our future. Greed is emerging as a prime mover in every strata of our society, eclipsing the virtues of public service. Intelligence is required to resist material temptations that are a subornation of honorable purpose.

In order for our nation to endure and flourish we need a new call to duty at every level. The best examples of service are dedicated elements of the military, committed members of the uniformed services, bus drivers, concerned physicians and many others frequently unrecognized and unappreciated in the day to day swirl of events. But they are only a small portion of a population suffering growing detachment from day to day responsibility for the condition of our nation. If there is still a best and brightest residing in our borders, they must be convoked to prepare a plan to fulfill the pledge of the Declaration of Independence, the constitution, and the promise of America for all its people, before it is too late. We may no longer be able to marshal resources, physical and mental, that compare with World War II, but we must identify and develop an elite, based on merit, to guide us through tomorrow.

An Assertion of Poetry

More than fifty years ago, at the age of sixteen, I began writing poetry. My first efforts were imitations of the Romantics; Shelley, Keats, Byron, my favorite, who brought order and structure into my chaotic life. School so far had been depressingly sterile, offering me little in the way of knowledge that I could not glean on my own, even less exciting was the pathetically sterile challenge of learning. So without a guide to direct my efforts, I plunged into the English Classical poets, having already read diversely in English drama and American fiction. I had memorized large chunks of Byron, Grey's Elegy and many others who delighted me, which was consoling as I struggled to find my path. After careful reading and evaluation of my poems, I found that I appreciated the developmental process, but concluded that they were wanting in originality. I burned them ceremoniously and reassuringly, this did not launch a career of book-burning. I did not regret their destruction and never looked back and said: 'If only I had saved them'!

I moved on to reading the American poets and devoured Eliot, Pound, Cummings, many others, who I found more timely than their English predecessors, sometimes almost as elegant, but never as beautiful. Beauty seems to be less compatible in the torment of the industrial age. Then, at the age of seventeen, I hitchhiked to California. I lived in San Francisco and discovered the Beat poets, who were just erupting in the formerly more tranquil landscapes of literature. I admired their vitality, but was turned off by their colossal naiveté. One of their loudest voices proclaimed that he saw the best minds of his generation destroyed by madness. I knew the best minds of my generation were preparing to send men to the moon. An immense and irreconcilable difference of opinion. Their movement offered me no safe harbour.

For the next few years I kept the semi-noiseless tenor of my ways, finding college almost as drab intellectually as high school, with virtually everyone focused on career. Whatever happened to the love of learning? Several slightly compatible companions helped keep me anchored, which let me endure in the wilderness of poetry. I, an emperor of impracticality, wanted to be a poet. I dreamed of tasting the immortal fire. I was ill-equipped for the academic environment, the protected haven of many poets, so I wandered aimlessly in an unknown land. One of the few benefits of my education was enough mastery of french to read the symbolist poets, then the more moderns, particularly Mallarmée and Apollonaire, from whom I rediscovered the invention of free verse. (French also allowed me in later years to translate Moliere for my theater work.) I read more and more of the younger American poets, looking for kinship. At the same time, I read the Russian, Japanese and Chinese poets, always feeling that the language barrier mandated translations, which altered the fabric of the writing. I began a search for my natural voice, an aspiration that imposed strenuous difficulties, since I was on my own and had to reinvent the wheel daily, a complicated task when working without blueprints.

The more American poets I read, the less connected I felt to their concept of poetry, however much I admired their artistic accomplishments. I saw a world aflame with constant upheavals, disasters man-made or natural, and progressively more destructive violence. Yet I found poets increasingly seeking esoteric metaphors, cherishing style above substance, placing form above content. Suddenly, all the poets were college graduates, many with advanced degrees in the field of poetry. I definitely did not belong in that company. I was the classic loner, but was sufficiently self-sustaining, or ego-driven not to seek entry into the networks of poetry. There was a corresponding classic irony. I, the consummate outsider, had been a theater director for most of my adult life. I had started in theater at the age of seventeen in San Francisco, plunging into an arts discipline that mandated group involvement! I found a curious symbiosis to the world of poetry, since I translated and directed the classics, as well as writing and directing new plays that dealt more and more with political and social issues. My poetry began to reflect the broader range of world problems, with the subject being my primary concern, not the expression thereof. This further distanced me from the practitioners of the art of poetry.

As the years went by, I found myself more concerned with the message, rather than the 'poetic' quality of poetry. I saw the arts begin to turn progressively inward, not in the nature of profound meditation, or seeking deeper understanding, but more in the aspect of flaunting personal agonies and confessions. This is what our culture has wrought. It satiates the consciousness with an endless stream of pictorial imagery that stupefies the visual sense and degrades the uniqueness of verbal description. So poets, increasingly shunted aside by a growing public preference for non-stop tv, turned to baring their guts in anguished revelations of childhood abuse, or indignation for their neglected feelings. This type of indulgence and I are incompatible. To me, poetry is greater than my personal sufferings. I feel there should be room in the chambers of poetry for alternatives to academic products and disclosures of angst. I have chosen my own direction and have evolved to expressing thoughts and feelings about issues. And if I may have abandoned metaphor and simile, it is not that I despise them, but I must deliver what I believe to be a necessary blunt message. In an age of increasing insecurity and danger, we must still cherish poetry. But the guardians of the gates of poetry should allow examination of the problems of the world, with direct communication, in order to extend the diminishing influence of poetry on the events of our times.

Globalization: Plan or Plot

The illusion of freedom is a dangerous deception that effects many educated Americans, insufficiently aware, if at all, of the feral nature of our capitalist based system. Corporate megaliths. gone global, are increasingly abandoning the façade of responsibility to national interests. The welfare of American citizens is of little or no consequence to the mostly anonymous dominant stockholders and corporate officers, whose only concerns are for the well-being of their vehicles of capital. When a corporation becomes diversified internationally, so that the course of local events does not interfere with over-all profits, the concept of domestic obligation is no longer valid..

In feudal times, one's masters were known, perhaps even susceptible to a petition of grievances, or a request for redress. The lords ruled their holdings, small or large, for their own advantage, not for the benefit of the people. Yet the crafts and tradespersons, progenitors of the middle-class, understood the system and however reluctantly, accepted their place in it. In the information age, the lords of profit are mostly removed from pubic access, shielded by great wealth and the power to control the content of the media. Their immense resources allow them to select politicians to reassure the public that we live in a democracy. But it is closer to reality to conclude that we live in an oligarchy, where policies are determined by a small cabal that are not necessarily in the public interest.

The twentieth century struggle for equitable allocation of resources between management and labor has been resolved by outsourcing blue collar jobs, or obsolescing workers by using electronic technology. The workers who once answered the call to strike, walked the picket line, confronted scabs, fought company goons, endured hardships to obtain a fair share of the American dream are virtually extinct. They have been replaced by lower middle class computer specialists, strategically divided by cubicles that discourage unity, or low wage service personnel, insufficiently equipped by education or inclination to influence policy. Yet the media and our leaders persist in proclaiming that we live in a democracy.

In a world still consisting of nation-states, each concerned with national interests, globalization only benefits those who gain from the diffusion of capitol. The average citizen will receive a lower standard of living. The disadvantaged will have few alternatives to low paying service jobs. When American oligarchs were confronted with foreign competition in the 1960's, they packed up their cash and went abroad. They chose to invest internationally in advanced industrial enterprises, pioneered in Japan, Germany and other innovating nations. They left rust belts behind for their former employees and families, because it wasn't profitable to retool obsolete factories, burdened with high labor costs, that now could be dispensed with.

The complex economics of Globalization make it exceedingly difficult for the average citizen to intelligently decipher the benefits and disadvantages accurately. Certain facts have become clear. Those capable of participating in the dispersal of capital and business will profit from the new opportunities. The diversification of capital will reduce the assets of middle class Americans, as the playing field they were accustomed to is leveled to allow for newcomers abroad. This will result in lower incomes and diminished opportunities for a better life for their children.

The working poor and disadvantaged will also suffer as the American tax base declines, thus reducing funds for social services and other supplemental assistance. The loss of support will not be compensated for by private charities and foundations with their own mission agendas, who will not dispense funds mainly to support a poverty population. The working poor, struggling to subsist on low-paying service jobs, will not have the resources to better educate their children to prepare them for the opportunity to compete for a better life. That opportunity will now be offered to select third world children, beneficiaries of the new global system.

American corporations are increasingly seeking tax shelters abroad. The reality of our economic future is painfully obvious in a simple premise. Reduced corporate taxes, plus reduced income taxes, minus increasing government and personal expenditures, equals disaster. Limited groups and individuals will profit immensely from the global marketplace. The American middle class, that once luxuriated in amenities that were formerly for the privileged class, must now make do with less. There is little doubt that Globalization will benefit many people in third world countries who can take advantage of the new world economy. Since capitalism is never concerned with ethics, the harm done to the American way of life has become a moot issue. It remains to be seen if the benefits of the Information Age will accrue to hard working Americans, who may not be qualified for the jobs of the future.

A Little Common Sense

America's porous borders are hardly an obstacle for those intent on entry, regardless of motive. It is self-evident that monitoring the borders and regulating entry is not among the higher priorities of our politicians and the bulk of our population. Despite the fact that it is an erosion of sovereignty, certain lawmakers and lobbyists have committed to a policy that weakens control of the access process at our borders. This allows unregulated participation in the benefits of residing in America without concomitant responsibilities. The concern for criminals or terrorists entering the country in the general illegal flow of aliens is obviously also not a high priority, otherwise urgent steps would be taken to close the corridors of vulnerability. Apparently the only way we will discover if weapons of mass destruction have been smuggled across our borders will be by a surprise disaster.

It is estimated that as many as twelve million illegal aliens, now referred to in order to be politically correct as immigrants, are in the continental United States. According to the media, several hundred illegals are apprehended weekly. This reporting is an attempt to convince the susceptible that the forces of law and order are still functioning. The disparity in the number of persons entering and those captured and deported, most to rapidly return, is enormous. This presents convincing evidence that the system is not working. There is a rumor that some elderly members of Congress dream of the regulated era of entry at Ellis Island with nostalgia. Granted that we face what seems like endless demanding problems, foreign and domestic, but the potential threat that hostile aliens present requires much more attention from our beleaguered government.

Since it is preposterous to imagine that our constabulary will round up millions of illegals, which is far beyond our allocated resources and political will, the conclusion is inescapable. We must establish a process that will quickly and efficiently legitimize millions of illegal aliens. Emergency efforts must be utilized to screen millions of hard working people and prepare them for citizenship. They should be encouraged to become

Americans and participate in what still could become a great society. They could be educated to cooperate in identifying dangerous individuals or groups who will threaten our nation. The alternative is alien residents forming alien communities, isolated from the mainstream of American life, further conducing to the fragmentation of our society

This large population group of newly hatched citizens must be allowed the same opportunities of ethnic immigrant groups past, to succeed or fail in the new country. Their children have to learn English as a first language, which will facilitate their participation in our society. Accepting their speaking Spanish at home, at school, in the workplace and in various transactions of the electronic age, further isolates them from the mainstream of the life around them. It also tolerates the establishment of alien enclaves, often in slums, that may or may not assimilate in the next generation.

The twentieth century saw a great population surge from the countryside to the cities. It is estimated that by 2020 almost half the people of the world will live in cities. If we don't want America to be a nation of festering ghettos, barely containing alien and non-english speaking dwellers who have no investment in the American way of life, we must institute a policy that compels the children of immigrants to learn English, not by fear of the bayonet, but by peer pressure from other youth, the same way children of immigrants past became part of our future.

The threat to national security increases daily, as the world learns, courtesy of CNN and other media, how porous our borders are. If we legitimize millions of aliens currently living under the constant danger of discovery, disruption of their fragile constructed existence and expulsion or incarceration, we not only remove an alien sea for enemies to shelter in, but we also enlist citizens who will share a mutual concern for our future.

It is possible that weapons of mass destruction have already crossed our borders and are in the possession of hostile extremists, determined to destroy our way of life. It is distressing that there may not be an emergency program under development to detect weapons of mass destruction already in the United States, which should have the highest national priority. It is even more disturbing that we leave our borders on land and sea open to the introduction of weapons of mass destruction. Protection of the homeland is a complicated and sophisticated task, but that protection must begin at home. Our vaunted technology did not defeat insurgents in Iraq, or Afghanistan. It is our soldiers and marines who may help impose a negotiated solution to a seemingly impossible situation. Our technological efforts should be focused on homeland security, before we suffer irreparable harm.

Thoughts on the Arts

An interesting phenomenon of the 70's was the byproduct of the Cold War between the United States and the Soviet Union, the culture war. We sent them rock and roll groups and Hollywood films. They sent us the Bolshoi Ballet and the Moscow Arts Theater. A curious exchange between the superpowers. Culture in the United States exists on many levels. Except for middle class adventurers who will seek the new, the experimental, the classics, wealth dominates all arenas, save theater. Opera, ballet, classical music, are funded by government and private donors. They are invariably not-for-profit endeavors whose mission is to provide the highest quality of performance achievable.

The peculiar nature of fine art is so removed from performance requirements that it exists in its own unique plane. Only the rich can afford to buy masterworks, though the public can visit well stocked art museums and see fine art. The problem is that most of the public have no idea what they're looking at, evinced by their rapid transit through display galleries. The public is invariably intimidated to go into commercial art galleries, a condition encouraged by protective art gallery personnel, who assume the public are not customers, ergo of no interest. It's even more difficult for the artists. Once it took a long time to become an old master. Warhol, Lichtenstein and a few others did it in record time, their paintings commanding multi-millions, pressuring art students, who may not be taught that there is room at the top for only a fortuitous few.

Theater is by far the strangest endeavor. Broadway productions are a financial venture that are only incidentally exercises in art. The cost of a Broadway production is so high that the goal is to produce a hit that will run a long time, repay the investors, then make a profit. Obviously this is not an arena for experimentation. Production values are generally high, but content, designed to reach mass audiences, tends to become safer and safer, the more production costs soar. The bread and butter of Broadway are musical theater and the most successful are revivals, or shows with familiar stories, made more glamorous by their history.

Off-Broadway production costs are becoming increasingly expensive. Capital investment is required to present a play that must earn money, or suffer a financial loss that ends the show. Regional theaters must cater to its subscription audience, a graying group, not readily replaceable. Off-Off-Broadway is usually a yell-in, or so sloppy that only Momma loves it. There are a few good small theaters that try to produce entertaining work, but their audience is also aging rapidly. At a recent Saturday night performance of a classic at a respectable small theater, the house was only ¾'s full and the average age was 65.

American theater, suborned by middle of the road university theater department mentalities, correlated with the deleterious products of the superficial show case system, has further fallen victim to increasingly visual improvement in tv, nourished by cable and the internet. When hi tech movies are added to the mix, all these formats combine to obsolete theater.

Alarm Bells Are Ringing

In the 2008 presidential election year the two party candidates carefully avoided any of the unsettling realities that might have jeopardized their chances to attain our highest office. They offered no answers to the loss of productive jobs, because they had no satisfactory answers. When American corporations were allowed to move capital abroad, instead of being required to reinvest at home, our industrial base contracted, then virtually evaporated. The substitution of low paying service jobs for higher income blue collar and small business positions, ended middle class aspirations for many. This condition established a second world standard of living for a large segment of our population, deprived of opportunity by the corporate desire for higher profits. New industries that will strengthen our nation and provide our citizens with production jobs is one way to raise our standard of living, rather than see it continue to become lower.

Presidential candidates now require hundreds of millions of dollars to present their personae to the electorate. Most of that money is provided by corporate investment to secure future cooperation from grateful recipients. Different levels of funding apply to all aspirers to office. The higher the office, the more money is required to sell the candidate to the public. The concept of grass roots candidacies due to prodigious cost, with the exception of small town Selectmen, is as obsolete as the biplane. When Ralph Nader continued his campaign for the presidency, he was blamed by many liberal democrats for Al Gore's loss to George Bush. This is a testimony to non-democracy, when only two political parties are considered acceptable to those of the liberal persuasion. We can only conclude that the good of the nation is not the first consideration from many of the suitors who purport to serve it.

As our economic woes continue to grow, a mortgage crisis that already has cost one million families their homes, threatens many more families, yet our candidates did not made it a priority to demand urgent home owner assistance. Some short sighted citizens say families who can't pay their mortgages deserve to lose their homes. In a nation of decreasing earnings, diminishing industries and an economy critically dependant on consumer spending, the forced departure of families from their homes will deplete the national tax base and reduce family spending. This further burdens the tax payer with the cost resulting from the loss of homes that could have been prevented. Bailouts of failing companies to preserve the stability of the economy is not unusual. It is also important to bail out large segments of the population for the sake of the economy. We are approaching a state of dire emergency and the candidates discussed certain issues that may be vital, but shouldn't be exclusionary.

The costs of the occupation of Iraq were not being shared by our putative allies, despite the fact that if we succeeded in establishing democracy in the mid-east it would benefit them. So the already overburdened American taxpayer must support nation-building, while at home our economic base is eroding. Our future president, whoever he or she may be, is not presenting a new initiative to involve our allies in sharing the cost of the reconstruction of Iraq. Our blood and treasure was expended to provide a new government with security as it rebuilds a nation. Were this venture to succeed, it would possibly transform the autocratic states in the mid-east that do not address the needs of most of their citizens, from exporting terror to importing the benefits of globalization.

America can no longer afford the simultaneous costs of being an international policeman, preparing for the next major war by developing enormously expensive hi-tech military platforms, and sustaining a population confronted with diminishing economic opportunities. It is purposeless to ask: 'Who owns America?', because the answer is simple: it is not the people. The citizens who were taught to believe in the constitution have been betrayed. At election time their votes are sought. Otherwise, they must fend for themselves in a society dominated by powerful corporations whose concern is profit, not the well-being of the people. Our prospective president depends on major contributions from special interests dedicated to profit, not the well-being of the nation. Our concerns for the future will be forgotten in the exigencies of office. As we aspired to build democracy in Iraq, we also required reconstruction of democracy at home. The American tragedy is that our leaders speak at the people, but do not work for them.

We are once again poised to accept rhetoric as an ersatz substitute for a viable action plan to regenerate the sagging fortunes of our people. We desperately need new jobs that will stem the submergence of the middle class into second world subsistence and offer better opportunities than service jobs. If the candidates cannot offer meaningful answers rather than campaign promises, we must learn to recognize that we are being misled. Of course universal health care is urgently necessary. But how will it be paid for? The government doesn't have the money, while the candidates are spending millions on electioneering, not healthcare services. Americans are smart enough to recognize their problems, they just don't have the means for solutions. Instead of specifics, we are given sweeping generalities that will be easily forgotten when the realities of elective office emerge.

None of the candidates dare to tell the public that the war in Iraq ended in 2003. Then the battle for democracy in Iraq began. Common sense tells us that only those who benefit from war, desire war. If candidates object to fighting for democracy abroad, let them offer a sensible plan that will not require more sacrifice later. In short, we the people who are growing poorer, while the rich are growing richer, need more from our candidates to lead us out of confusion. The fervor that greets candidates is an indicator of our hunger for solutions to difficult, complicated problems. Speechmaking will not alter the reality that confronts America. We need constructive change, not superficial promises that excite, but don't satisfy.

Whose Land is It?

Frequent killing sprees, a growing poverty population, overcrowded prisons, a failing education system and fewer good job opportunities. Sound like a second world country? That's what is happening to much of America, except for the privileged caste. The once bright hope of the future of humanity, the formerly expanding middle class that realized the American dream, is now being discarded. After various historical struggles, the elements that combined to form a united, collaborative nation are being separated, not by race, creed, color or class, but by wealth. The process started insidiously in the early 1960's, when it became apparent to certain American corporations that their industrial processes were becoming obsolete. Instead of allocating the capital to upgrade, retool or completely rebuild, they found it more profitable to invest in their foreign competitors, abandoning any responsibility to America, leaving us the cancer of rust belts.

Great upheavals affected our society in the 1960's, the civil rights movement, the anti-Vietnam war movement, assassinations of our leaders, all set against the terrifying threat of nuclear annihilation in the Cold War. For the most part, these complex events were reduced to simplistic blurbs by the media, politicians and universities, secure in the belief that we were too burdened by day to day obligations so that we would only monitor the flow of events superficially. The sound bite became a primary information tool. And while we were struggling with the issues of white flight from the cities to the suburbs, we overlooked the insidious flight of capital from domestic investments to foreign shores.

The blue collar workers were the first targets of corporate deaccessioning. Their battles against begrudging management that frequently won higher wages and better benefits would not stop. The policy makers of the steel, automobile and electronic industries took no pride in their superior work force. It didn't matter that their workers were experienced and competent; they put a huge dent in profits. There was certainly no concern for the contribution the workers made to the economy, either in taxes or consumer spending. As soon as another option for investment was decided, the workers could be dispensed with. So the steel mills and factories began closing and the jobs went abroad. Yet no one alerted us that we were being permanently abandoned by the owners of our vital industries, whose obligations to profit took preference over the needs of the nation.

Our public education system, primarily designed to prepare our youth for factory jobs, did not evolve to discover alternatives while the factory jobs were evaporating. Somehow or other many of the crucial elements necessary to comprehend a difficult, complex world are not part of the educational process. The world began turning faster. Television showed us daily the goods and services that most of us hunger for. And unlike many human institutions, television doesn't discriminate. Its wares are broadcast for all to see. Only cost determines what we can get and in the process conditions us to desire what we are showed. And we still dreamed of a better life, not understanding that the corporations that don't care about us have ended many opportunities for a better future.

As computers took over industrial functions, the blue collar work force was further reduced, replaced by a new techno-class that thought itself indispensable in the burgeoning Information Age. The techs learned the hard way that they were as dispensable as toilet paper and easily replaceable. So the blue collar class was disappearing, the last organized component that possessed the will to resist the abuses of capital. Small businesses were being devoured by chain stores. Durable products were giving way to cheap substitutes manufactured abroad. The national debt became so enormous that we could no longer grasp its significance, let alone recognize who it benefited. The depletion of decently rewarding jobs was eroding the optimistic fabric of American life.

More and more corporations are setting up outposts abroad to avoid paying taxes to the government. The assault on high paying jobs continues unabated, leaving low paying service jobs as the main field of employment for most Americans. Our leaders still insist we are the richest country in the world, but as the lights go out in homes across the nation because of foreclosures, who will pay our bills? Recent studies indicate that we have more millionaires than any other country in the world. Once our pride was in having the largest prosperous middle class. Now we are fearful of the future and fervently respond to politicians who promise change, blindly hoping for a savior, refusing to accept reality. The pressures and tensions of our times are disconnecting many of our youth. The increasing suicide attacks on our schools, workplaces, shopping malls and restaurants is one small symptom assailing a diseased national body that urgently needs attention, before it decomposes. The changes we require are not empty promises from politicians, but a regenerating of opportunity for a huge segment of our population who are as American as the wealthy.

Is the Poet Obsolete?

The role of the artist in society has changed dramatically at various times in recorded western history. One of the earliest notable exemplars of the reputable place that a poet occupied in society is Aeschylus, who did his public duty in 490 b.c., when he fought against the Persians at the battle of Marathon, participating in the struggle for survival of the democratic polis, Athens.

The options of the artist diminished rapidly with the growth of empires, since the role of the artist is not vital to the existence of the state. For almost two millennia, the normal pattern of life for the artist was dependency on patrons, sponsors, or commissions. The exceptions were the select few born to privilege, for example, Byron, who gave his life for Greek freedom, perishing in 1824 at Missolongi, during the Ottoman siege. During this span, the artists outside the system led difficult lives and were fortunate to practice their art, however difficult the conditions.

The industrial revolution diversified the control of wealth by the lords of power, bringing forth a new class of financial barons, who turned to the arts in imitation of their betters. Suddenly artists were able to create their work without it being pre-sold, consequently they were no longer mere craftpersons. Many became personages of some stature in the eyes of the new prosperous middle-class society.

From the 1870's on, some artists had a world view that allowed them to look beyond their individual discipline, as they searched for a more significant role in the life around them. Poets patriotically enlisted in World War I, and the British poets in particular wrote about the horror they experienced. The poets who dutifully went to war in World War II returned quietly and never really developed a public identity. The crisis for American poets began in the early stages of the Cold War. American painters skyrocketed to world acclaim, fame, fortune, while the poets composed in relative obscurity. More and more poets sought a modicum of security, finding shelter in universities far from public recognition and reward.

In a dynamic American cultural revolution, every art form from the 1960's on, offered the possibility of wealth and status to the artist, except poetry. Poetry had no opera houses, concert halls, museums, galleries, or mass-market publishers to attract large audiences. But the poets now were college-educated and with a few exceptions, such as the Beats, led obscure lives in colleges. The artificial atmosphere comforted the isolated wordsmiths with the illusion of accomplishment, reaching small groups of students, readers of poetry periodicals, and miniscule audiences attending poetry readings.

Poetry in America experienced an identity crisis. The anti-Vietnam war movement in the late 1960's firmly closed the portals on the topic of war, mankind's most consequential activity, as a suitable subject. Virtually all American poets were liberals and in all good conscience opposed war, so the government became the enemy. Since the poets mostly could not identify the capitalist owners of America, they scorned the system of flawed representative government and retreated further into safe niches. Internal revelations and lurid exposés of parental abuse became valid subject matter, transforming the nature of poetry into microcosmic excursions, rather then explorations of big issues.

In an era of uncertainties and dangerous conflicts, domestic and foreign, there is no designated role for the artist in American society. The very concept of training poets in college, an environment that discourages extremes and negates any natural inclination to action, leaves the poet adrift in a world that dismisses the practitioners of passivity.

The poet travels towards his or her destination, a journey of creation of what should be a meaningful body of work, through a haphazard combination of education, exposure and personal preferences. This occurs in an unstructured process that makes the accomplishments fortuitous. In medicine or engineering, students are taught and trained by measurable standards and the results are assessable. Even acting, the most superficial of the performing arts, which lacks the stringent requirements of music or dance, has more predictable goals than poetry. The poet's path could be adventurous, since it explores an uncharted wilderness without landmarks or traveler's aids, but it will be a dismal voyage for the timid.

Poetry, once the preeminent literary art, has been supplanted by mass market commercial fiction. The authors of novels have become far more prominent than any poet, whose limited possibilities of achievements are determined by effort, talent, and coincidence. Rarely is anything meaningful achieved without a mentor, the sponsorship of a like-minded network, or a supportive artistic community. The poet can be susceptible to a stifling tendency to huddle together in protective enclaves, rather than move in the sphere of the world at large.

The poet must learn to expand his or her perception of existence and enlarge their scope of interest, or risk becoming inconsequential in this demanding life. There is an urgent need to reach out to diverse audiences, prisoners, seniors, the culturally underserved, and most important, to youth, not to make them poets, but to introduce them to a broader view of life. With proper instruction, poetry is the most accessible and cost-effective way to reach large numbers of youth. The constriction of the classroom rarely develops confidence in youth, the quality that allows them to choose who they will grow up to be. The poet can help launch venturesome journeys for youth that will promote their contribution to the future of our society.

It is implausible that America will produce warrior-poets who will fight on tomorrow's battlefields of freedom. But those poets who wish to participate in the life of their times, participate in a grander arena of creativity, design a meaningful role for themselves in their society, must outreach to needy and deprived audiences. The poet's efforts will enrich their audiences, who in turn will reward those poets who are receptive with the great satisfaction derived from serving humanity.

The Alarm Has Sounded

More and more Americans are struggling to make ends meet as we experience a severe economic crisis manifesting indicators that it may get much worse. During the great depression, despite the tremendous disruption to the economy, the nation still had a vast industrial base as a foundation to allow recovery. Today we are no longer an industrial society. The millions of blue collar jobs that were the backbone of the nation no longer exist. In the 1930's, when government initiatives developed public works projects, this was a temporary fix until the economy rebounded and once again long term jobs were available. This facilitated the climb back to prosperity.

The current situation requires urgent attention, since people are losing their jobs, homes, savings and any hope of security in the future. Individuals are not losing their jobs because of the failure to be productive. They are victims of a negative element of our system that has abandoned its hard working citizens, who relied on their government to protect them from failed or failing rapacious corporations, whose obligation is to stockholders, not the well-being of the people.

The dismal performance of the banks is due to rampant greed, fiscal mismanagement, or diminutive intelligence. Totally irresponsible lending practices, made to borrowers with insufficient collateral were a major cause of the current recession, which is threatening to become a depression. After incurring enormous financial losses because of unsound practices, the banks, exercising the power of special interests that influences congress, persuaded the government to bail out the failing enterprises. Congress allocated billions of dollars of taxpayer's money to save the banks from their own mistakes. Yet despite receiving public funds, the banks continued to foreclose on homeowners who could no longer make mortgage payments. To add further abuse besides the injury done to those evicted, the banks used bailout money to reward management with substantial bonuses and other expensive perks.

There is a Kafkaesque scenario in banks taking money from the people to reward those who failed, while the very same failures are evicting people from their homes, instead of bailing them out. Accusations of this abuse of the public trust as being 'shameful" is an ineffectual excuse not to take action against the violators of the public trust. Our system should not allow the exploitation through either malice or greed aforethought by the banks. In the least we are entitled to a legal investigation into what is moral turpitude and may well be criminality. White-collar crime may not arouse the same horror and repugnance as rape and murder, but a violent assault has been committed on the vulnerable by exploiters who took public money, evaded accountability, conspicuously consumed the money, then punished the very people who provided the money.

Our leaders seem to overlook both the cause and effect of these reprehensible actions. There is no demand for restitution of misspent funds, nor insistence for a freeze on foreclosures. The banks are not providing credit to the small businesses that are dismissing workers and losing income. Large corporations are cutting thousands of jobs, an event that will disable the diminished blue-collar class and remove a skilled pool of workers from any hope of labor participation in industry. The middle-class is being disassembled, since large segments are no longer able to earn a sufficient income in the dissolving economy. Arbitrary corporate enactments are dissolving the futures of millions of Americans.

Our citizens aren't ignorant peasants to be brutalized at the will of feudal lords. They are vital contributors to the fate of a nation and are entitled to protection from the lords of capital by the duly elected representatives of the people. The complexity and demands in this life mandate reliance on officials, elected and appointed, for guidance and solutions to the vast scope of problems confronting the nation. The custodians of the public trust are obligated to special interests in order to attain and retain their offices. There is a fundamental conflict between the oath of office and actions that contradict it. The rights of the people do not correspond to corporate profit-making. The people are entitled to special protection against special interests.

The concept of spending on public works to create jobs to stimulate the economy is only viable as a transitional program that will lead to long term employment. Our diminished industrial capacity will not provide opportunities and growth, consequently the current plans for economic recovery are at best a temporary alleviation, not a solution. We need a major commitment of funds and effort to explore new industries that will provide long-term development to stabilize the nation and offer rewarding employment to our citizens. We urgently need to invest in new technologies that will replace moribund industries with innovative enterprises that will contribute to the well-being of the nation.

To Be or Not To Be…. Better

In a period of severe economic downturn, education will suffer from declining funding, like the rest of a struggling society. Until there is a revolutionary change in educational philosophy that will downsize the arts and promote math and science vigorously, the role of arts, fine and performing, must be examined to assess its practical application in the classroom.

It is critically important to evaluate the potential achievements of the individual arts in order to determine what to discard and what to retain under the pressure of budget cuts. If the standard for consideration of the importance of the arts in the curricula is defined by measurable results, it is necessary to objectively apply the accomplishment of tangible goals that have maximum effect on large numbers of students.

This essay is not an aesthetic comparison of the arts, but a utilitarian guide to the most efficacious application of a meaningful learning tool. Music and dance require the development of high skills for any significant progress, therefore they are not ideal vehicles for transmitting the benefits of the arts to numerous classrooms. The fine arts of painting, sculpture, etc, are also technically demanding and are appropriate to special talents, not the general student population.

Art appreciation is a wonderful means of stimulating the learning process, enhancing a student's life and inculcating a desire for culture. Without extensive preparation that presents the nature and structure of the arts, minimal exposure will only reach a small percentage of the student body. Appreciation of the arts is highly desirable in a culture overly focused on television and computer games. However, it may be an unaffordable luxury, compared to the retention of teaching jobs.

One of the most, if not the most important requisite for the student is the development of confidence. This characteristic enables positive participation and exploration of the learning process. With a carefully designed syllabus, supplemented by appropriate teacher guidance and encouragement, drama can be an ideal method to help construct the willingness to explore new subject matter, without the fear of failure that often restricts student's efforts. The process of getting up in front of one's peers and overcoming inhibitions will result in improved academic performance and the acquisition of general life skills.

Students should not be encouraged to become actors, directors, etc. They should be urged to become willing participants in an experience that will help them overcome fears of inadequacy and low self-esteem. The benefits of functioning in the public spotlight will be apparent in improved grades, positive attitudes and better involvement in the learning process. This will be facilitated by the teacher expressing appreciation for efforts, not comparisons to others, or for their talent as actors. Drama can easily be incorporated in the curricula to include difficult or underserved students.

The major reasons for selecting drama before the other art disciplines, are: affordability, since no elaborate supplies are necessary for basic classroom activity; accessibility to all, regardless of differing levels of talent and ability; active involvement in a dynamic process that precludes passive participation; the development of a mindset to overcome obstacles and explore risk-taking without negative comments or criticisms; the application of a tool that is all-inclusive and will contribute to creating a positive environment for learning.

Any good teacher can easily prepare to use a dramatic methodology that will outreach to all, rather than appeal to an elite by rewarding the facile or talented few. Since our society doesn't test infants for their future potential and opportunity is more available to the privileged, the educational system is vital in the development potential of the majority of students. Our society faces innumerable problems, including fractured families and the overexposure of youth to television as an early learning mechanism, not the ideal educational process.

The responsibility of preparing youth for their roles in society mandates their nurturing and the educational system is the crucial environment. Our future existence as a culture will be determined by the success or failure of our students to become productive citizens, who will solve the problems of tomorrow.

Raw Realism, a Poetry Manifesto

The nature of poetry has evolved since the innovation of free verse and now should allow vast latitude of expression. Too many self-appointed guardians of the realm of poetry presume to righteously define the boundaries valid for exploration, arbitrarily excluding what may not appeal to their particular sensibilities. When some of the French Symbolist poets, in particular Rimbaud, Mallarmé, Apollonaire and Valery, shattered the forms used for centuries and created free verse, resistance was automatic from the academics who scorned them. Those poets are venerated today as a vital part of literature.

The last major disturbance in the tranquility of poetry was caused by the Beats, who were dismissed as ill-disciplined, ill-mannered, disreputable advocates of sex, drugs, and rock and roll. Now they occupy a respected niche in the cathedral of poetry, having survived alienation from the mainstream despite excursions in autonomous verse, or unrevised stream of consciousness ramblings. Their contribution exploded some of the restrictions on style and content, but their accomplishments have become stratified, while their disruption of incipient ossification has been forgotten. They are now as tame as Byron, Keats and Shelly, other forbearers who lifted the torch of rebellion against arbitrary constrictions on subject matter.

Traditionally, the self-anointed custodians of verse attempt to regulate the form, style and content of poetry and deny the validity of differing efforts. Many of the janissaries of poetry, sheltered by universities, grants, or private support, reject the adventurous spirits who seek other directions. The issues of our times are at least as consequential as effusive celebrations of the seasons, laudatory odes on public occasions, or indulgence in self-absorbed introspection.

The ancient Greeks raised poetry to the acme of public attention, with presentations of poetic drama at annual major festivals that were socio-religious-political-artistic competitions, with a laurel wreath for the winner. Today the most energetic presentations are poetry "slams", crude performances of diverse material in rapid transit deliveries that contradict the fundamental needs of poetry; careful attention, time to consider the meaning and an atmosphere conducive to understanding, rather than raucous burlesque.

The only way to sustain poetry in the Information Age and maintain its relevance is to make it meaningful to audiences conditioned to the internet, ipod, Blackberry and text messaging. The dictum: "Form follows function" is still pertinent. If the duties of the poet can be conceived to include chronicling our times, protesting the abuses of government, raising a voice against injustice, speaking out about the increasing dangers that threaten human existence, it is critical to allow substance not to be shackled by style, content not to be constricted by form.

Rhyme and meter were once the only practiced format of poetic expression. Now they are increasingly marginalized. Perhaps metaphor and simile are not more sacred. We must aspire to emotionally engage new audiences, involve them in the illumination that poetry can transmit, preserve the existence of a vital form of human expression that is being overwhelmed by a saturation of easily accessible, diverting entertainment. We must also develop new voices that may achieve a dynamic readership by offering an alternative to brilliant wordsmiths. We need poets who will offer meaningful and significant truths to a public saturated by confusing information and nearly jaded by ongoing visual assaults on their sensibilities.

The Myth of Democracy

Ancient Athens has been hailed as the birthplace of democracy, with good reason, as long as it's understood that it didn't mean liberty and justice for all. Governance of the City-State represented a colossal achievement in history, heretofore characterized by rule of chiefs or kings. In the 'Golden Age of Athens' there were 25,000 citizens. The rest of the population consisted of peasants, trades people, slaves. There was no standing army. Citizens armed and trained themselves for the defense of the state from threats, notably the Persian invasion, thwarted at the battle of Marathon, 490 B.C. When a tyrant usurped the rulership of the governing class, supported by a personal bodyguard, it took a while to throw off the oppressive rule.

Athens was the first state to be ruled by the people. Of course it was restricted to certain people, the wealthy, the influential, the privileged, those able to use the system for advancement. Almost endless litigation went on and the lawyer class was established, sophists able to equally argue both sides of an issue. But people sued each other, instead of killing each other. Without the Athenian innovation of the rule of law for some, the development of civilization could have taken many millennia.

The Roman republic attempted to adapt many of the Athenian examples of governance. But just as Athens succumbed to a policy of conquest and expansionism, so did Rome. The patricians of wealth and power usurped the rule of the Senate, determining policy, foreign and domestic. They allowed a large underclass to pressure the system with unruly demands, that they resolved with bread, circus, or violent suppression. When power was finally centralized in an Emperor, everything else became subordinate to the imperial prerogative. Conquest and expansion built an empire, more civilized than the rest of the world, but autocratic. When overexpansion and many other causes led to collapse, the 'Dark Ages' followed, because there were no institutions to take Rome's place.

Organized civilization began to arise from a period of chaos and disorder, and the feudal system evolved for protection against Viking incursions. Despite the theory of obligations both ways, the demands of those above always took precedence over the needs of those below. Nobles called their underlings for service, which had to be obeyed. When Harold Godwinsson destroyed the Norwegian Vikings in 1066, at the battle of Stamford Bridge, the noble class was so established that they continued a system of obligations to the high-born. The struggle for the rights of the people went on in England for hundreds of years, culminating in a limited monarchy that allowed the people some rights, but governance was still in the hands of the rich and powerful.

Like Athens and Rome, the British Empire expanded through conquest, cloaking many invasions under the pretext of bringing civilization to the natives. The Industrial Revolution put England ahead of every other nation in wealth and power, which facilitated the further growth of the empire. Yet whatever system English masters introduced to their native subjects, it was unacceptable foreign oppression, proven by the rejection of British rule when it could no longer be enforced by power. Yet mechanisms of democracy were left behind, even though they were dominated by the rule of power, wealth and privilege.

The American Revolution, led by a small group of men of wealth and privilege, threw off what had become oppressive foreign rule. They produced what many believe are the most wonderful documents in history, The Declaration of Independence and the Constitution. This unique rejection of monarchical rule, with promises of life, liberty and the pursuit of happiness affected many with the vision of freedom. And the owners of the new nation had only stolen a small portion of the vast continent, mostly from Native Americans, but from anyone else who stood in the path of expansion. But there was room in this new land for common people to blaze new trails, carve homesteads, farms, towns, out of the wilderness, as long as they were willing to kill the previous owners of the land. And they felt independent. Except for slaves, bound people, lackeys, many people felt free. At least until civilization arrived with the demands of law, taxes, military service, which paid for the enormous resources needed to steal a continent.

Then democratic America stole a big part of Mexico. The hunger for land drove people westward and as they had since the first landing on the Atlantic coast, intruded, negotiated, bartered, killed all those who stood in the way of expansion. But the Eastern magnates had grown strong enough to challenge the Southern agricultural barons for control of the nation. And a great divide opened between the owners of the land. The inevitable clash saw the Industrial North master the art of modern war, outproduce the more rural South and beat it into submission.

The end of the war between the states set millions of restless men, tested by the rigors of war, adrift in an unsettled land. The rush to claim farm and ranch land from native Americans led to bloody conflict, small in scale after the ferocious war that devoured the blood and treasure of the Civil War. Settlers paved the way West, supported by the army, in a now unified nation dominated by industrialists eager for new markets, with vast resources yet untapped. Within a few years, Native Americans were reduced to reservations and the land began to fill up. We bought or stole all foreign held land, so the owners of America began to look abroad.

The Spanish Empire was crumbling within and without, so the venturous capitalists daringly turned their sights on foreign conquest and acquisition. With the usual superficial motives to conceal crass greed, war was provoked. Young, energetic America overwhelmed creaky old Spain and not only stole Cuba and Puerto Rico, to dominate the Caribbean, but captured the Philippines, thus becoming a Pacific power, which was linked to the annexation of Hawaii and Guam.

Then American democracy tried to digest new conquests, make them part of the nation, even though they were offshore, far away.

After all, we grabbed Hawaii and that was offshore, far away. But the Filipinos didn't want us. Neither did the Cubans. And they resisted the benefits of democracy, at least the capitalist kind, despite benevolent efforts to impose the lot of little 'Brown Brother'. Only Puerto Rico didn't fight our occupation, hoping to gain peace and prosperity from imperialism.

It took a while for the owners of America to accept that they couldn't digest Cubans or Filipinos, or exterminate them, or confine them to reservations. To end continuing bloodshed, independence was promised down the road. We didn't worry about their future then, because we were adept at promise breaking. But we didn't know what to do with Puerto Rico, so we left it dangling, with an inconclusive status. Now that we were masters of countries in the Pacific, the Caribbean, we need a bigger navy to patrol, control unruly elements that might interfere with commerce, intrude on our self-proclaimed sovereignty, rebel against our authority.

Our burgeoning industrial might stirred more ambitions. We were too late to stake claims in Africa, already divided among the big dogs of Europe. We were too late to stake claims in Asia, already divided by the big dogs of Europe, as well as Japan, emerging as a power after defeating Russia. So we snuck in with lofty proclamations about an 'Open Door', since we weren't strong enough to demand a share of chunks of China. Yet when the resentful Chinese took up arms agains the sea of invaders, we always sided with the imperialists.

The European powers built great armies and navies to maintain empires and defend against belligerent neighbors. So when Germany, come later to imperial land grab then France or England, ringed in middle Europe by unfriendly nations, was determined to expand, conflict became inevitable. The Generals who planned the Great War were still fighting wars past and did not comprehend the democratic power of the machinegun, which devastated huge armies with countless casualties. And the owners of America watched from the sidelines for several years, while the Great Powers drained themselves on Western battlefields, as well as much of the rest of the planet.

The warring powers, weakened by years of the loss of men and treasure, were finally ready for American intervention. Our troops fought on the great stage and acquitted themselves creditably, but when it came to establishing the peace, the old dogs outsmarted the young pups and we went home seemingly without profit. Yet everyone owed us a lot of money for selling them war materials that they didn't have the cash to pay for. We cleverly introduced the dollar as the new world currency, replacing the Pound. But we learned how to discard Civil War mentalities of how to fight, and some Generals prepared to fight a modern war.

American corporations thrived in poor Latin American countries, dominating the one product economies with total control, reinforced by the Marines, whenever the locals resented our democratic exploitation. And we watched cautiously as Germany rebuilt and Japan started conquering China, selling them raw materials to nurture their war machines, until their expansion threatened our interests. So after selling Japan steel to build her ships, planes, tanks, we cut off the sale of oil that they needed to run them. This was an almost forgotten episode, except by some historians, some of whom think we forced Japan to attack us in order for them to seize oil fields to fuel their military.

So we fought another great war across most of the earth. After waiting long enough for Europeans to deplete themselves, we responded to Japan's attack on our territories with the greatest industrial output in history, producing huge amounts of war materials to provide to our military, as well as our allies. At the end of World War II we were the big dog and we briefly dominated the world. When Communism resisted capitalist encroachment and established a rival empire, a competition was born. The 'Cold War' stimulated our industry to produce more and more war materials, as well as domestic goods, allowing middle-class luxuries never imagined before and blue collar aspirations for their children to live better.

The owners of America were not content with millions. They wanted billions. But factory workers with salaries and costly benefits, ate into the profit margin. So when the aging factories needed upgrading, they were abandoned, along with millions of workers, for factories abroad, with cheap labor, thus allowing huge profits. Entire regions were devastated by corporate departure, leaving rust belts as a reminder of capitalist selfishness. The American Dream was callously removed from the future of discarded workers and their families.

The 'Cold War' was a great benefit to the owners of America. The military/industrial complex thrived to nourish the legions that occupied much of the globe. The technical race to produce superior new weapons brought vast profits to the arms makers. Production of domestic goods poured into every home that could afford them. And more people could afford them then ever before. And education flourished. Thousands of colleges turned out hundreds of thousands of graduates, many of whom contributed to the growth of the economy. Except for a few dangerous confrontations with the Russians that might have incinerated much of the world, America seemed to be relatively safe.

The Vietnam incursions started with a handful of advisors, then grew and grew until it dominated the American psyche. It took a while for anti-war fervor to rouse enough resistance to government policies for the media to turn against the war. Youngsters 'turned on, tuned in, dropped out' and wanted to make love, not war. Protestors divided the nation. Yet the owners of America let the war go on until swollen with profits they ended the carnage. But the nature of American life had changed. Patriotism was no longer a dominant force.

A new breed of citizen opposed government and corporate actions that hurt the people, the environment, cause after cause, issue after issue, disrupting the tranquility of the lords of profit. With so many alienated from 'traditional' values, the middle-class agitators became dispensable. The blue collar class, the only group that fought the bosses, was deaccessioned first. The factories that hadn't closed or moved abroad, turned to automation, which removed human jobs, increased profits by eliminating costly labor and depleted the unions until they could no longer demand, only request benefits from the bosses.

Large segments of the middle-class were no longer needed, since they didn't comply with the objectives of the owners of America, whose capital was so diversified that they were no longer dependent on domestic consumption for their profits. When the Cold War ended with the collapse of the U.S.S.R., American investors filled many gaps that the Soviets could no longer afford. But enemies were always needed to justify maintenance of the war machine and stimulate patriotic loyalty in support of one's country. Cuba no longer stirred the people to anger, since without Russian missiles it was merely a semi-tropical backwater. But the Middle-East was ripe for exploitation.

The only way a dominant military could benefit capitalism was if it made war, necessitating all the costly materials of war, as well as selling materials to friends and enemies. So we invaded Iraq in a massive campaign that didn't change anything, but generated huge profits. Not all our citizens seemed to realize that as the self-appointed policeman of the world, we only patrolled certain beats. We continued making big bucks supplying arms to our allies, South Korea, Japan, others, keeping potential future customers, Vietnam, The Philippines, for another day. The Asian market was relatively profitable and stable, so Europe and the Middle-East were priorities. We welcomed new members to N.A.T.O., and their business, also continuing tensions with Russia as we encroached on her old empire and resources.

We conquered Iraq again, then saw the country dissolve into warring factions. Then we did the same thing in Afghanistan. Critics argued we were failing at state building, but stable regimes were never the goal of capitalism rampant. Chaos and war is much more profitable. At home, a vocal minority, in defense of democratic values, objected to government policies with little lasting effect. The blue collar class was virtually powerless and could only support the bosses, though not overtly, or see their remaining factories immigrate to a more profitable clime, Much of the middle-class was becoming expendable, since enough wealth was concentrated in the 1% that a large consuming class was becoming obsolete. As income declined, less was spent and small businesses and stores began to close.

The ascension of President Obama filled the liberals with hope, but they never inquired where half a billion dollars came from to elect him. He was probably the least experienced candidate in our history, but he did a credible job, continued the wars in Iraq and Afghanistan, sent tendrils into Syria, maintained tensions with Russia and China, kept the wheels of business and industry turning. And if Republicans were outraged at his health care act, their outrage kept many focused on a domestic issue that mattered little to the owners of America, as long as the public didn't meddle in net profits and foreign affairs.

Historians may wonder one day how the most unqualified candidate ever defeated a slew of Republicans all more experienced and qualified. Then, with the help of Russia and the F.B.I., Trump defeated the most qualified candidate since George W.H. Bush. Trump's character and pronouncements outraged a lot of Americans, who protested volubly, a few violently. Many intelligent citizens joined demonstrations opposing objectionable policies. But in America, the rule of law is controlled by the system, regulated by elected officials indebted to their funders, so their obligations to the people are secondary, if they want to continue in high office, the cost of which is paid for by the owners of America.

For a short time after World War II our people were lulled by comforts, at least some of them, since capitalism requires a poverty class to exploit as needed. The children of the parents of comfort actually believed they were democratically entitled to resist the abuse of power by their government. Objectors were so busy protesting the war in Vietnam that they didn't notice the removal of the industrial heart of America, which went abroad. When citizens finally realized their children would not lead better lives then their parents, many resigned themselves to diminishing opportunity. The Information Age is not for masses of the population. The Service Industry is the future for many. Only strong pressure on the owners of America can compel the trickle down of material prosperity. Only well-paying jobs can restore a prosperous middle-class. Unless there is a new, innovative age to gainfully employ many, the American Dream is rusting away.

What Level Destruction?

Many world mythologies include a goddess dedicated to chaos and death. These deities may represent a fundamental element in man's make-up, the urge for self-destruction when unable to cope with the conditions of life. As man evolved, moving from primitive to barbaric, codification began to establish rules and customs to mitigate against a harsh existence. When empires replaced tribes as the primary organization regulating public and private activities, law initiated a gradual strengthening of human rights, which became a socially desirable norm with the emergence of the nation-state.

Democracy, certainly one of the most complex institutions created by an ingenious species, offered citizens protections that actually brought reasonable prosperity and security to more people than any former type of government. Yet like all human creations there are always imperfections. The American experiment purports to be a classless society, as implied in the constitution, but is as stratified as any class society, merely lacking formal titles of distinction. The class differences between American capitalists and other lords of commerce or nobility are miniscule. They are all characterized by the drive for acquisition, the maintenance of wealth and position, the amassing of goods and services and the typical lack of association with those less well off, the underclass.

Throughout history, the development of communications fostered extreme change in the normal framework of day to day existence. The advent of television initiated a long term seduction of the human psyche with visual tantalizations denied to the lower economic strata. The constant proffering of temptations that ultimately entered every home, assaulted viewers at every level, depicting what they could afford to acquire, as well as tormenting them with the unattainable, except for the privileged few.

Many men, perhaps not as far removed from brutal beasts despite the trappings of civilization, develop frustration levels from thwarted desires that under certain pressures drives them to explosive violence, without regard for the consequences to others.

The frequently occurring acts of apparent senseless violence and murder are becoming increasingly an accepted norm in our conflicted society. Several particularly alarming trends are multiplying: the angry boyfriend murdering the girlfriend's child; the rejected lover or husband going on a homicidal rampage; the disaffected loner planning and carrying out slaughter. There are many other symptoms that reveal the mental and emotional illness pervading our society, but the examples cited are extremely disturbing because of how often they manifest themselves, briefly and traumatically shocking the nation.

It is a cultural aberration to murder a child out of misplaced rage or frustration, yet our society lacks an effective preventive system. A society that cannot protect its children demonstrates a dwindling survival quotient. Our system has proven unable to identify the threat to vulnerable children and successfully intervene to insure their welfare. Media announcement of another child victim has been a weekly event. When a man cannot accept rejection from a woman and retaliates with a murder spree it often includes innocent bystanders in the home, workplace, school or church. This not only is an indicator of diminished intelligence, but a virtually primitive reaction to intense frustration levels, kindling rage that bursts into violence inflicted on others. Yet these same individuals came through our school system without identification of their earlier problems, or amelioration of their potential homicidal tendencies, when under severe emotional stress.

The calculating loner, abandoned by either parents, school, friends, a nurturing system, or a combination thereof, surely displays symptoms of disaffection, but they either go unnoticed or untreated. The suffering individual seethes, until rage boils over. He invariably plans an assault that maximizes the damage he can effect and often includes sealing escape exits. He erupts in a controlled frenzy, determined to take as many companions as possible with him on the sudden journey to death. The event also results in the attackers suicide.

Despite lurid media exposure that ultimately stupefies the senses, we still react with horror to these dreadful crimes. The increase in murderous rampages culminating in suicide is supplemented by increasing media coverage of traumatic events that are allowed to disappear when audience attention turns elsewhere. We easily become inured to tragic events by excessive media exposure, consequently causing growing indifference to violent incidents. This reduces our emotional response and depletes the stock of public indignation to request policies that will redress grievances, before they explode into tragic episodes. .

The peculiar conditions of American life, great latitude and great constriction, impose numerous obstacles to simple solutions for complex and controversial problems. The need to prevent incrementing violence is urgent, but there are many restrictions on actions that might be efficacious, yet violate current laws, affect the requirements of special interest groups, or offended the public's sensibilities. However, we seem to confront exponentially multiplying threats to the well-being of individuals and the state. At the same time, civil rights advocates resist implementing surveillance of public spaces, fearing encroachment on hard-won civil liberties. Since there is an unwritten code of public behavior accompanying the laws regulating public behavior, some question why this is a controversial issue. Advocates seem to be defending the right to commit anti-social or criminal acts in public, without being officially observed, under the aegis of non-government intrusions on the right to privacy. The concept of privacy in public is contradictory.

It is painfully obvious that only early intervention might prevent the development of significant behavioral disturbances that later surface in murder. Whether we have the skill and the will to do so is a debatable issue. In the Information Age, ever-increasing access to weapons of mass destruction through the internet, especially chemical or biological, should warn citizens that we must be better educated and more involved in the recognition of warning signs from disturbed individuals threatening to detonate. The relatively easy access to certain chemical and explosive weaponry, such as anthrax, or homemade bombs, should alert us to the growing need to prevent destructive incidents, rather than react after the fact.

The most alarming characteristic of the individuals who run amok is in their drive for self-immolation, they want to take as many victims as possible with them. If we accept the possibility of a highly intelligent simmering individual of this type acquiring a weapon of mass destruction, there is no doubt that he will use it, in some cataclysmic event that will result in a maximum of harm. This person may have already been born in the U.S.A. and may already be on the road that will lead to disaffection, resulting in calamitous destruction. A functional domestic intervention program should be urgently developed to avert a possible massive tragic occurrence.

Heartless, Thoughtless City

The egregious policy of evicting homeless families with children from city shelters for real or contrived offences is a violation of the basic human rights of the victimized children. There is no alternative provision of services for the evicted children. Where are they expected to live? Eat? Receive vital assistance? Why has the city neglected to consider their needs in the haste to dismiss troublesome parents?

The city already has the authority to eject single men from shelters. We can only hope they would deal kindly with veterans, who have done their duty for their country. The necessary power to evict families with children required state approval. It is no surprise that the callous collaboration to evict helpless children between the city and state was supported by elected and appointed officials, a shameful enactment. The entrenched bureaucracy is indifferent to the fate of homeless outcasts in a bureaucratic system that is long on official indifference to the unfortunate homeless and short on compassion.

It is heartless to put children on the street. Regardless of the offenses of the parents, the children require care and attention, like any other children. These children should not be punished for the infractions of the parents. The sins of the fathers may have been the judgment on the House of Atreus, the House of Laius, but we are supposed to be a socially caring nation. Do the officials who decide the fate of these children have any idea what their lives are like? It certainly appears that they are unconcerned with their fate.

It is thoughtless to perpetuate the offense of the parents on their children, who have little chance to escape the destructive influences of homelessness that crushes their lives. These innocent victims will be blighted by the official abandonment, followed by the resultant suffering and horror that are conditions of homelessness. Someday these children will repay our society with crime and violence, a probable alternative to the failed hopes for a decent life, prevented by official neglect and rejection.

The homeless, who are not a constituency since they are not legal residents in temporary shelters, are deprived of civil rights that many citizens take for granted. The children of homeless families experience their own particular deprivations. They are not welcome in the local school districts, where they are an additional burden on middle-class sensibilities. The negative environments of harsh shelters, unfriendly schools and hostile communities combine to shatter the future expectations of homeless children. Eviction to the streets reflects the moral bankruptcy of government enactments without conscience.

The Rampage Syndrome

Homicidal rampages are occurring more frequently in America. Each incident is followed by extensive media coverage that numbs the public psyche with panoramic details. Interviews with emotionally tormented survivors, grieving family members, friends and surprised neighbors moderate the horror. Officials with endless explanations or statements of consolation dilute the significance of the event. Police authorities invariably discover the immediate background of the rampager, identify the means used to carry out the drastic attack, while expert consultants suggest possible reasons that motivated him.

The loss of loved ones is an anguish for the bereaved, but at the same time lawyers immediately estimate the economic cost of loss for legal claims to come. The cost of emergency response by police, fire, and appropriate government agencies is enormous. The disruption to normal functioning might go on for days, or longer, another blow to an already distressed economy. The resulting trauma from the attacks on those involved may go on for years, draining the ability of those affected to work and enjoy life. The cost both to the individual and the public is extensive.

Many of the attacks are characterized by cunning, but limited to remedial planning. A target, chosen for a particular reason, is selected and an assault is prepared. The assailant arms himself with the most effective weapons accessible. He often wears a bulletproof vest, an obvious indicator of a desire to resist the anticipated police response as long as possible, since he is already decided on suicide. He explores various means and devices to control the target environment. These incidents demonstrate that rampages have escalated far beyond someone reaching for a gun in a moment of rage and shooting the supposed cause of his provocation.

We should accept the existence of an evolutionary process that translates an individual's rage into a more sophisticated conception of revenge. We can conclude that the attackers are becoming cleverer in their preparations and more destructive in carrying out their intentions. We may extrapolate that a highly intelligent, disturbed individual with a broader hunger for vengeance, as well as access to the internet, may devise an attack to redress grievances on a scale hitherto confined to the worst terrorist scenarios. Yet this may be an emerging reality that should be considered by any sane society intent on the preservation of its citizens, property and institutions.

If we accept the premise that a violent, disaffected individual might become the author of a massive attack on a vital industry, an important research facility, a military installation, a major city, we move beyond police jurisdiction to the arena of national security. We learned to accept "going postal" as a social norm. We classified the unibomber as an unique phenomenon. The anthrax sender has virtually been forgotten. The current category of death wish seekers taking others with them is becoming a standard occurrence. The potential for the combination of the suicider with the means for mass destruction is a dreadful possibility that must be addressed by responsible authorities.

Recent events indicate that schools follow the workplace as the frequent targets of disturbed individuals with a grievance. If we factor in religious extremists, with the potential to collaborate with terrorist organizations, we can perceive an ongoing threat that will continue to escalate. The malady that causes suicidal rampages is a virulent disease that inflicts America and may escalate into an epidemic, if not addressed.

How do we protect the nation from these traumatic assaults that have even reached into the reasonably controlled world of military bases? Should we accept these losses as part of the price of democracy, since they are so limited compared to the fatalities of drunken driving, which we don't prevent? Can the danger of attack increase until the threat to many warrants police state like profiling, surveillance and monitoring? When does the menace grow so perilous that it justifies extreme protective measures?

In an economy that has lost millions of good paying jobs, most not to return, a collaboration between government, academia and the private sector can create a new industry, rampage prevention. We have not learned the harsh lesson that incarceration does not prevent crime. We must alter the mindset that creates a penal industry that produces nothing, merely warehouses over two million felons, while only generating custodial jobs. Rehabilitation is a negligible result of imprisonment. Therefore, we must develop new methods to deal with crime and violence, or continue maintaining expensive, non-productive storage facilities.

We experience limited deaths today from disturbed rampagers. It is not unreasonable to postulate that massive destruction tomorrow is a distinct possibility. In a nation with an overabundance of deranged citizens, implacable enemies, porous borders and endless internet tutorials in methods of mass destruction, it is logical to conclude that we must develop protective means, or risk the terrible consequences.

Half measures are insufficient to preserve a stable future. Reactions after the fact do not prevent or deter new assaults. We require protective measures that effectively identify, locate and apprehend those intent on destructive rampages. A major project should be inculcated to develop the means to appropriately detect potential threats before they occur. This will require an enormous effort politically and socially to apply hard and soft science, as well as other pertinent means, to forestall disasters. The loss of a large city to biological, chemical or nuclear attack will make the expenditure of resources cheap at the price. It is imperative that our elected officials and citizens determine to face a dreadful problem that threatens us all.

The Evolution of Poetry

Once rhyme and meter were the standard format for poetry. Great poets, Shakespeare, Shelley, Pushkin, Lermentov, Baudelaire, Poe, T.S. Eliot, exemplified the style of expression. Many 19th century poets stirred the passions of avid readers not yet detached from the urgency of poetry. As major forms of communication multiplied more and more rapidly in the 20th century, the role of the poet as a voice of his or her times began to dwindle.

The poets who saw combat in World War I, shocked by a level of destruction not seen before, were the last link to generations of poets who wrote of the horrors of war in traditional forms.

The advent of radio began the process of removing people from the written word. Motion pictures accelerated the pace of change, adding dazzling visuals, then an incredible range of sound. For the first time, people could sit back and spectate in the isolation of the passive environment of movie houses. Television, the most powerful tool yet disseminated to shape the human mind, provided escape from reality in the privacy of one's home. The ready access to non-stop programming allowed absorption in a conditioning process that altered the nature of viewers, especially children, who were encouraged to stay indoors and watch tv, rather than go outside and play.

Poets began losing their sense of identity, in a society that had an overabundance of cultural opportunities for diversion. Poets struggled to find a niche in the artistic fabric of creativity that was now dominated by visuals. The last clear poetic exception to the omnipresent pictorials was the 'Beats', who became identified with the anti-Vietnam War movement. However talented some of them may have been, they were perceived as against 'things', rather than inspiring a challenge to the establishment to improve. Many readers overlooked their brilliance, instead focusing on what they perceived were whines and complaints. This was a poor conclusion to the historical march of what appears to be the last defined group movement in American poetry.

The Information Age allowed the proliferation of on-line literary magazines, many aspiring to the achievements of their print forbearers. With the advent of thousands of magazines, many edited by younger people eagerly expressing lofty ideals, countless poets found ready acceptance. Many literary magazines offer contests, for a fee, that attract poets willing to pay for the privilege of belonging to a cultural milieu. Consequently, much of the effort to publish poetry by income oriented editors encourages poets who value the arbitrary acceptances beyond any meaningful worth.

This is an era of declining interest in the arts, theater, ballet, opera, classical music, all affected by dwindling audiences. It is a peculiar phenomenon that on-line magazines are multiplying at an astonishing rate statistically. For every one that closes, two more open. Many print publishers are forced to move further away from literary books, by necessity publishing commercial books, or perishing. Only the University presses and stalwart literary magazines continue to maintain their role as print publishers. How long they will continue, depends on economics, rather than dedication to literary excellence.

So where does American poetry goeth? When we factor in the visual domination of the educational process at home and at school, youth are conditioned early along pre-determined paths that are not conducive to constructive introspection. In the course of time, many thinkers believed that the true artist was born, and the coincidence of life allowed development to a mature expression. Our college classrooms are filled with poetry majors and the democratic process insures 'equal treatment'. Many students go on to get advanced degrees in poetry. Colleges may teach technique, but they are not exponents of unbridled passions, formerly the fuel for poetry.

Poetry is the most solitary creative process of all the arts. It is also the most fragile, so far removed from large audiences and public renown that it is inexplicable why we have so many poets in America. They far outnumber engineers and chemists. Our society does not seem to have the capacity to elevate a poet to be a culture hero. So what is the role of the poet in an electronic world of instant communication? Poetry is closest to theater in ideally providing the audience with an emotional experience. But unlike theater, the poet rarely impacts well through performance, but through receptive reading. Poets once inspired, illuminated, seduced, possibly stirred to wrath, all emotional extremes that justified the exertion of the isolated artist. The movement away from live performing arts is implacable. In a superficially conditioned visual culture words cannot compete with hi-tech imagery. Nevertheless, the poet must continue to present a humanistic element in his or her creative process, otherwise the poet will become increasingly divorced from the issues of our times, and lose relevancy.

Bullying, A Preventable Disease

The need to stop bullying with its injurious mental, emotional and physical effects, takes priority over explorations of the root causes, or examination of why perpetrators engage in negative behavior. Several horrible incidents ending in tragic suicides have dramatized the seriousness of the problem. This resulted in brief government attention to educator's responsibilities to prevent harassment as required by federal law.

The Department of Education issued a letter clarifying the legal responsibilities of authorities in public schools, colleges and universities under federal laws, reminding them that certain kinds of student bullying might violate federal anti-discrimination law. This legal caution to educators is an evasion of responsibility to the victimized students who are not receiving protection from assault, while educators are being advised of legal statutes, rather than how to formulate prevention plans to protect their students.

Research by the Department of Education in 2009 revealed that one-third of all students ages 12 to 18 felt they were being bullied or harassed at school. This is not only a confession by the educational system that they are not protecting the rights of our children, but it is a statistical admission of a pandemic. Instead of an urgent summons to action to cure this disease, educators are being warned to comply with their legal responsibilities. Once again the interests of the bureaucracy are being given priority over the needs of the vulnerable students, as well as their concerned parents.

Bullying, whether it originates in nature or nurture, certainly begins before children attend school. Our government is virtually powerless (or even capable) to intervene in the home and offer moral instruction, or introduce the concept of respect for the rights of others. This was formerly the job of parents and the duty of religious institutions. Judging by the staggering number of afflicted children, the development of responsible behavior at home or in houses of worship has been ineffective or neglected. Consequently, the seeds of bullying, sown before pre-school, are already rooted when regular school commences.

Between divorce, the decline of church attendance and increasing public controversy about gay issues, the traditional developmental process of youth has been altered. The only remaining institution in American life with any conceivable possibility of stabilizing youth and encouraging a positive learning process is the educational system. Educator's, both teachers and administrators, must be trained to recognize the changes in youth that make them more insecure and uncertain in dealing with the demands of life. In an emergency, the medical community, the government and the public is mobilized to deal with a contagious disease. Similarly, educators must be prepared to fulfill functions that were once the responsibility of other institutions. The well-being of our nation may depend on how we address the critical need to equip our children for the problems of tomorrow.

By the time a child is 12 years old, behavior modification is only possible with intense personal attention by caring teachers, supplemented by confidence-building activities. This is impractical in a system that is already struggling to meet innumerable demands on its time, resources and personnel. A further complication is the questionable willingness of many individuals to give the requisite support to children. In a system characterized by overcrowded classrooms, a lack of individual attention and opaque educational goals, it is imperative to properly prepare children in pre-school or kindergarten to respect the rights of others and encourage them to explore their talents and potential abilities in a protected environment. The current focus and controversy over gay student harassment is incidental to the problem of bullying, which existed before gays were an acknowledged component of our society. Due to complicated legal, moral and social considerations, the gay issue is not readily resolvable in the classroom. Bullying is.

One possible solution is instead of encouraging our best and brightest to join the Peace Corps, we should urgently recruit a dedicated group of caring, young teachers to participate in reinventing the early developmental process. This will protect our children and allow them to build a better future for themselves and our society. Another option would be to include an accredited how-to college course for teachers in identifying and preventing bullying, regardless of race, creed, color, religion, intelligence, or sexual persuasion.

In order to establish a bully-free environment both in classroom and playground, children must be instructed how to rechannel negative behavior impulses, as well as taught how to deal with confrontational situations. Since bullies invariably select weaker targets, it is imperative for teachers to protect their charges and teach them how to resist bullying, or how to request adult help.

In nature, the stronger establish dominance over the weaker and rule by virtue of their physical authority. Humanity has aspired to substitute intelligence for strength, using tools, weapons and machines to exert control of the environment. It is a contradiction of both individual rights and society's needs to allow oppressive children to intimidate smaller, weaker, generally more intelligent children, stifling their natural development. Just because a child is weaker, it doesn't mean they lack pride, dignity, talent and unmeasured potential to develop skills and ability to enrich our nation. The harsh assault on their sensibilities destroys self-confidence and impairs the willingness to risk active participation in the learning process. These traumatic experiences lead to low self-esteem and result in a lack of self-worth that inhibits new explorations, a vital stepping stone to future achievements.

We must urgently recognize that our society values brawn over brains. This is demonstrated in elementary schools, where bullying is most often carried out by the more athletic boys, on the weaker, more intelligent and smaller boys. This iniquitous imbalance progresses through high school and college, where the jock is admired and the scholar is ignored or scorned. We are not able to calculate how many children never developed their potential talents or abilities due to early intimidation. But it is imperative for us to understand that however much our citizens appreciate athletics, it is at best a distraction from our national needs, which mandate applied intelligence to confront the massive problems challenging our existence as a first world country.

Children are our most precious resource for tomorrow. Yet we carelessly or indifferently waste their potentially vital contributions by mentally, emotionally, sometimes even physically, allowing them to be crippled by mindless assaults from unrestrained bullies. The long term effects of bullying are debilitating and can cripple the mental and emotional development of vulnerable children. The school system is the only hope of protecting our innocent children and nurturing their potential. Yet many teachers appear to be oblivious to the oppression that goes on about them. Teachers are the only possible doctors and nurses to treat the disease of bullying. They must be trained to identify, then modify the behavior of bullies, while recognizing the children who are victimized and teaching them to seek help.

Our teachers are currently unprepared for this formidable challenge. They or their union are insufficiently aware of the dire need for action, while many are indifferent to the consequences. That is why we require a dedicated corps of younger teachers, a special forces-like unit, to urgently combat the epidemic of bullying that not only takes place in the classrooms and playgrounds, but in hallways, or right outside the school. We desperately need more intelligent citizens to create a better future for us and our descendents. We have excelled at making money and war, but our scientific and technical achievements are diminishing, while the arts and sports are expanding. Our continued well-being mandates math and science for our survival in a competitive world. A crucial battlefield is in pre-school and kindergarten. We either recruit compassionate warriors to fight for our children, or continue to contribute actively to the brain drain that will bankrupt our nation.

Where Have All the Classics Gone?

In the early 1970's, Off-Off Broadway theater expanded rapidly, fueled by hordes of recent theater majors seeking performance outlets. Dozens of small groups presented an incredibly diverse scope of productions of highly mixed quality, from the imaginative to the excruciating. Few groups lasted more than a month or two, attributable to the basic fact that they were unprepared to deal with the reality that theater is a business.

Many inexperienced young actors and directors, who had no concept of their theatrical limitations, talked art day and night, but did not grasp that money made production possible. Without cash, there is no continuation of artistic purpose, since sweat equity efforts last only so long and the demands of day to day existence compel young practitioners to move on.

Because America never had a national theater, there are no measurable goals for young actors and directors to aspire to. Unlike opera, ballet and classical music, with their rigorous requisites for performance, theater is a haphazard amalgam of temporary relationships and there are no universal standards of requirement for performers. Selection of casts and directors takes place through loosely related networks, word of mouth, and auditions in response to ads in the trade papers. Casting, a speculative process at best, generally offers no dependable levels of accomplishment suitable for the demands of classical theater.

The absence of theater education in grade school and high school, except for the privileged, along with the commensurate lack of exposure to live performance, does not build a widespread theater audience. Deadly exposure to Shakespeare in the classroom inflicted on students without tools to grasp the language and history, makes classical theater virtually inaccessible. The school system designed to develop appropriate skills for factory labor with the goal of job readiness in an industrial economy, cannot conceive that properly presented, theater can be practiced by anyone, regardless of talent or ability, as long as the purpose is to build self-confidence and self-esteem, rather than turn out hordes of performers. Music and dance mandate an early start in training, hard work, lengthy practice, intense instruction and technical mastery. The lack of these requirements for theater provides youth an excellent opportunity in school for personal development, using theater as a mechanism to build self esteem and self-confidence, when properly encouraged, to get up and do things in front of others. The absence of these requirements for professional actors is one of the many factors that has contributed to the decline of classical theater.

Actors tend to discover theater in college or university, ten or more years after musicians and dancers began their training. Colleges took control of actor training from the professional theater in the mid-1960's. This legitimized the once disreputable profession by bestowing aspiring actors with a bachelor's degree in fine arts. The emergence of regional theaters, invariably affiliated with a well-endowed college, bewitched masses of drama students enchanted by the state-of-the-art theaters. Enthusiastic local audiences encouraged student actors into believing their future would take place in equitable surroundings. Trained in sophisticated and protected venues, outside of the safe haven of the university, the students were woefully unfit for the harsh realities of the Off-Off Broadway theater world.

Theater education now firmly embedded in the college system, flourished academically, providing comfortable livelihoods to legions of teachers and administrators who would otherwise intermittently wander the unpaid wilderness of small theaters. The standards established by the classroom advocates were sufficient for actors intending to seek work in film or tv They were woefully inadequate preparations for the classical actor, who needed the same basic discipline and structure that would be the equivalent of music or dance training.

Another factor diluting serious theater was the graying of the current audience, without a new demographic audience to replace them. When adventurous classical theater lovers ventured Off-Off Broadway to see Moliere or Sophocles, they generally encountered an awkward, arbitrary updating. Deconstruction of the classics, advocated for student directors by many drama departments, invariably eliminated the class distinction of the original drama, the fundamental structure of the classics until Ibsen. This democratization removed kings, princes, barons, fatuous lovers, scheming servants and great issues, reducing the scale of drama to middle class reenactments. To add to audience travails, performances were often offered as a shouting match, rather than a dynamic, well-presented period play.

The further erosion of the actor's potential was facilitated by the implementation of the showcase system. This was an ill-considered collaboration between the actor's union, an organization characterized by 95% professional unemployment of its members, and producers. This travesty of the arts stipulated three unpaid weeks of very limited rehearsals and three unpaid weeks of performances, for a total of twelve, on three successive weekends. The showcase code specified that the actor could leave the show anytime for paid work. Forgetting the risk to the producer, who could lose his lead actor to a margarine commercial, as well as his investment, the superficial preparation for Macbeth or Othello guaranteed a dismal performance. Unlike opera singers or ballet dancers, who maintain roles in repertory, the actor learns a role during brief, mostly discussional rehearsals, frequently resulting in mundane superficial recitations, rather than exciting shows.

The advent of cable tv, with hundreds of shows and thousands of roles, eclipsed the lure of the classics by offering the actor paid work, audience appreciation and recognition. Technological advances in filmmaking eliminated the appeal of theater's feeble efforts to compete with spectacle. Audiences conditioned by the big screen, were disappointed by shabby productions, often clothed by the same old costumes from the Costume Collection, on the small stage. Mega-musicals were the only type of theater production that still attempted to dazzle the audience with special effects. The scale of production was necessarily reduced for touring, to the disappointment of local audiences. At the same time, the Broadway musical audience was diminishing in numbers.

Theater had forgotten its key historical ingredient that riveted audiences since ancient Greek drama; intense emotional experience conveyed by the quality of the play, and the skills of the actors. With regional theaters spread across the country disseminating shows tailored to the tastes of their local community, and Off-Off Broadway testing the limits of small audiences, the classics were in severe decline. Classics were less frequently produced on Broadway, and when they were presented it was invariably as a star-vehicle, generally without a strong supporting cast. Audiences quickly discovered that a star alone cannot enliven a Shakespeare play, let alone the lesser known plays of Aeschylus or Racine, who are even more alien than 'old Will', who bored them silly when they were forced to read Shakespeare in high school.

It is improbable that the disappearance of classical drama as part of American cultural life can be halted. The only remote possibility would require a zen-like flash of enlightenment in the members of the college theater departments; emotion and highly skilled actors are the tools to engage audiences. If we are to retain classical theater, actors and directors not only need to be trained appropriately, they must be cautioned that there is little fame or fortune compared to movies and tv. Few actors would be willing to devote themselves to the intense training required for the classics for meager rewards. Audiences offered endless entertainment, will not accept poorly produced theater. The visual spectacle of the big screen is the final undoing of the classics in America

The Greater Need

Homelessness is a national problem, most apparent in cities with their more accessible resources for basic survival. Two particular categories of homelessness should require priority of services from government and private agencies: Families with children, who are innocent victims; veterans who have served their nation and are owed a debt of gratitude for their service. This selection of target sub-groups is not to dismiss the needs of other homeless, but offers a definition of our triage obligations when not all can be given the services they need.

The children of homeless families, frequently headed by a single, dysfunctional mother, are the most vulnerable youth population in America. They lack the basics of stability that allow normal development; secure home, safe and loving environment, healthy diet, belief in self-worth and a positive image of personal identity.

Too often, the homeless children are exposed to drugs, crime, violence, prostitution, and mental, emotional and physical abuse from out of control boy-friends. That our society allows these conditions to go on year after year in a violation of individual rights guaranteed by the Constitution of the United States amounts to crimes against humanity. Whatever the failings of the parents, the children should not be abandoned to a devastating existence in the present and dismal prospects for the future.

It is critical for the agencies and organizations dealing with homelessness to understand that a dysfunctional mother cannot be expected to function normally, merely by providing her with housing and a job. Since our resources are so limited, it is mandatory to implement a triage system that will target the most salvageable: children. The only way to stabilize a dysfunctional single mother with children is to provide intensive support services that will protect the environment for the children and allow them the developmental opportunity for a better life.

The providers of counseling and social services must recognize that the mother must be sustained in order to protect and preserve the children. The children should be considered the primary clients, with the mother receiving services designed to sustain the children. It is unrealistic and economically wasteful to expect a dysfunctional mother to improve without comprehensive individual services that our system not only cannot afford, but doesn't even believe are necessary. The requirements for acceptable job performance, limited subsidized housing, and paying rent for shelter accommodations, are not viable accomplishments, without extensive support for the mothers.

The current shelter system, supposedly a way station that should lead to permanent housing, does not address the urgent needs of children in their most formative years. These children, while isolated from the surrounding neighborhood due to the placement of shelters that are not rooted in the community, watch television, which accentuates what they lack. Without a nurturing substitute for what appears to be the normal lives of the children they see, but they do not have, traumatic alienation occurs, blighting any hopes of recuperation from the cumulative effects of homelessness. These children desperately need regular personal attention from caring adults, providing substitute parenting, guidance and positive development activities, designed to rebuild self-esteem and stimulate eagerness for the learning process.

The children of homeless families must be considered a potential asset of a struggling society, already diminishing in resources for the well-being of the nation. If the children's vital development is neglected, we will not only lose their future contribution, but they will become a liability, a burden that might have been averted. Perhaps more than any other youth population, these children are at higher risk of failure, due to their direct exposure to the most negative elements of our society that accompany homelessness. These children do not deserve to be discarded without the same opportunity as other children in America. The ability to insure their future is a problem susceptible to solutions by a concerned society.

The problem of dealing with homeless veterans is complicated by the to-date lack of recognition of our debt to them for their service. It is questionable how many of this troubled population can be salvaged and put on the road to functionality. But, they earned our obligation by putting themselves in harm's way, to protect us at home and abroad. It is crucial to remember that these vets were not policy makers deciding national issues that some of us might object to. They did not initiate war or launch attacks without government approval. They served, as police and firefighters serve, to help the public. Perhaps veteran's organizations, or other concerned groups might be induced to form a foundation that would sponsor permanent housing, with appropriate support services for these neglected veterans.

Despite the supposed best efforts of our government, federal, states and cities, homelessness has become more widespread. The economic downturn and the loss of millions of jobs will further result in an expansion of the homeless population. As a demographic group that does not vote, they are too often neglected by career legislators, primarily concerned with continuing in office. Diminishing resources make it easy for many to ignore the need to develop practical, humane solutions to difficult problems, contributing to terrible human suffering. We urgently require more creative and constructive solutions to the problems of the most needy homeless population.

Some Ask: What is Art?

When the Catholic church dominated Western Europe, depictions of the saints and other religious images were the only subjects allowed to be displayed. People had little or no trouble deciphering what they were looking at. This was one of the many artistic periods that the interpretation of subject matter was not in question. Everyone recognized the pictures that adorned churches or castles.

25,000 years ago, a prehistoric critic stood in the Altamira cave in Spain, and regarded renderings of bulls and other animals. He certainly did not say: "My six year old nephew can do better." 23,000 years later in the 19th century, the transition from realism began and separated the mass of people from the few who acclaimed the new art. Gone were the days when powerful prelates, rich noblemen and well-to-do burghers commissioned works of art from craftsmen. The age of the independent artist opened the portals of art to rapidly expanding methods of expression.

It took awhile for the public to appreciate the Impressionists and get over the shock of shimmering color and alien textures. But they finally recognized how non-threatening and sedate the movement was and it became a reassuring staple to a public slow to accept innovation. Then abstract art reared its confusing head and created a bigger gap between artist and audience, when social and economic changes allowed the public to view beautiful but incomprehensible paintings in galleries and museums.

The twentieth century brought the rapid and dynamic progression of different styles of painting, alternating realist and abstract movements that occurred more quickly, each stretching the visual comprehension of viewers. This created a self-appointed cultural elite who claimed proprietorship of the new art. A vocabulary of esoteric terms, some critical, some technical, further removed accessibility from the public.

Creative fervor exploded after World War II and by the 1960's there were so many explorations of new forms, materials and artistic conceptions that it was beyond the capacity of the average person to even follow what was being done, let alone appreciate wide ranging directions that pushed the limits of acceptance to all but a handful of art world insiders.

Historically, the passage of time permitted the public to grow accustomed to the artist's creations that once were alien, but ultimately became acceptable, even appreciated. A huge single color painting with one thin stripe was no longer viewed hostilely. Other artistic extremes moved into the realm of the normal, extending the conception of what was art. In an almost infinitely varied field of expression, former measurable standards disappeared. Artists produced work of such diversity that only the most controversial, such as the use of excrement as a material, could arouse the stupefied senses of an overburdened public insufficiently prepared to evaluate the range of artistic creation.

It is unreasonable, perhaps oppressive, to attempt to restrict the areas of expression the artist explores. However, there are some excesses that should be confronted by those concerned with the enduring nature of art. As long as the artist is not seeking to destroy the lives of others, or threatens the existence of legitimate governance, it is virtually impossible to confine the scope of individual creation. Yet at the same time, the lack of standards allows an artist to gain fame, fortune, acclaim, while exploiting public ignorance by covering the wonders of nature in stifling plastic.

The latest infliction on the vulnerable public is a 50 million dollar project that will drape fabric almost six miles over the Arkansas River, in Colorado, on a still moderately pristine canyon, home to bighorn sheep, the Colorado State Animal.

This installation of an unnatural element on a large swath of nature is an act of destructive vandalism, not artistic expression. The artist has a lengthy history of smothering nature's beauty with artificial material that only suffocates the subject of his sterile attention. If the artist covered garbage dumps, sludge pits, slums, strip mining, he would at least conceal the horrors mankind created. Instead he selects unsullied places for his attention, at prodigious cost, that neither enhance, nor improve the targeted site.

We can no longer expect art to be humanistic. Our visual, electronic culture dilutes the awareness of expression, once the realm of the creative artist, now dominated by film and tv. There should be a turning point, where intelligent culture lovers should reject the colossal deception of a meaningless body of work that fools many, due to endorsement by the few.

Cultural Speculations

The vision of American culture is inevitably tainted with advertising. Television is the medium that emits torrential commands to millions of conditioned viewers to buy 'our car, beer, shampoo'. Advertising includes the means of attenuating the minds of the public, which have been shaped into a sedentary mass no longer capable of resisting glamorous urgings 'to want'. There is a more frightening aspect of this brainwash. The standard home situation in which our precious sons and daughters, faces fixated on the television screen, our refuge, our curse, are reduced of the potential to resist the implacable demands to acquire goods. Even worse, those who cannot acquire goods legally, are more motivated to get what they want criminally.

Today, our scientists boast that we are dozens of years ahead of ourselves technologically. The few among us who point out that we are dozens of years behind ourselves morally, go unheeded. The disparity can lead us to impose a philosophic question: who should determine the fate of a large portion of the human race? The gross misuse of power in the hands of the avaricious is analogous to placing a number of children, with very sharp knives, in a small, crowded room, then the adults depart with the concerned admonition: "Don't hurt yourselves."

Our economy is manipulated by a small percentage of the 1%. What they don't need they can dispense with, despite irreparable harm done to millions. More profit desired? Close factories and ship them overseas. Personnel too expensive? Outsource them overseas. Unions costing too much? Bust them. Why should blue collar workers have security? Material comforts? And if they are strong enough to dispute issues with the bosses, they're an imposition on business and earnings, which won't be tolerated. So the bosses hire politicians to pass laws restricting union activities. Yet we're still encouraged to buy, buy, buy.

The children who have grown up in apathy, contributed by television values, will not rise up to protect their supposed rights under the constitution. They're too comfortable. The minor eruptions, like 'Occupy Wall Street', blaze brilliantly for a short time. Yet the protesters couldn't incite the public to support them because of confusing agendas, uninspired leadership and the inability to connect with the millions who lost homes, foreclosed when the Real Estate Bubble burst. The banks and insurance companies were bailed out by the government of the 1%. The millions who were foreclosed were just abandoned, and they didn't march on Washington, or even state capitols to demand justice. They just stayed home, until their homes were foreclosed, then hulked somewhere, watching tv. looking at all the treasure they couldn't afford.

A Fairness Manifesto

Capitalism, though less tyrannical than fascism or communism, is nevertheless an unmitigated enemy of democracy. The system that allows millions to do without, and the few to feast in the lap of luxury, does not serve the people. Unlike the role of a traditional aristocracy, vaunting superiority over the mass of citizens, in America the majority of citizens have been deluded into believing they are as good as anyone else. This is further enhanced by the hirelings of the lords of America, funded to gain elective office to serve their masters, while convincing the public that they represent them, not the special interests that spend millions to elect cooperative law makers.

One element of the success of capitalism is that unlike fascism or communism, the illusion of personal liberty is promulgated. Another device is the trickle down effect allowing middle class prosperity, and lower class access to credit for the acquisition of goods, at periodic intervals . When economic security, comfort and conveniences are abruptly removed, in what appears to be managed cycles of recession and depression, the public is manipulated into blaming one political party for the disruption, electing another to improve conditions. Yet each major party, despite alleged differences, are financed by the same funders who decide the policies of the nation, regardless of disastrous consequences to so many of our citizens.

The determination of the future of a society by an oligarchy of limited ability, besides the accumulation of capital, is an affront to the American ideals that millions have given their lives for, and to even more millions who were promised the precious commodity of hope. Were the owners of America benevolent, they would permit health care for a needy and deserving population, rather than enriching the insurance companies who have arrogated to themselves the determination of medical treatment. They would replace the outdated public education system, designed to create factory workers for factories that no longer exist, and prepare our children for a meaningful place in the future, currently only assured to the offspring of privilege, select athletes and a token number of the meritorious.

The list of debilitating problems confronting our nation is vast. Yet there should be no indictment of those who have more than others. That is an historical human condition. There have always been those who amass wealth, while the masses struggle to survive. The complaint should be lodged against those who have so much, yet will not contribute a fair share for the benefit of the majority. It can never be morally right in America that someone who has five Picasso's and three mega-yachts pays much less of a percentage in taxes then a working mother with children, who pays twice the percentage in taxes. Our system is even more corrupt than ancient Rome, where class distinction was endemic, since our society deceives with lofty ideals of the constitution, limited to the benefit of the few. The constitution is suspended for a single mother with children living in a homeless shelter. Here we feed the hungry on myths of equality. As long as the owners of America sate us with television entertainment in the isolation of our homes, at least the homes they allow us to keep, and allot some of us basic subsistence, they will continue to direct our existence to our long term disadvantage.

There is little to be gained in resorting to revolution to overthrow the capitalist system. As a people, we lack the wisdom and moral force to create a better system. Rather than besieging the gates of the wealthy to punish them for their economic oppression, which motivates the system to defend itself against irresponsible forces, we must find a practical method to compel the oligarchs to permit a fair share to all citizens. All Americans should have the opportunity through education and effort to better their lives. A new political entity, 'The Fairness Party', dedicated to abating the selfish tyranny of excessive wealth, should be founded. The member's first commitment will be to request legislation that allows a fair chance for all to participate in the American dream.

Insourcing/Onshoring

Year after year, the virtually uninterrupted flow of drugs across U.S. borders created a dedicated culture of users. This infliction on our tolerant republic has been reinforced by glamorous films and tv shows that constantly illustrate drug use. It has become an American norm to get high. As the volume and variety of narcotics consigned to our country increased, so did the incomes of all participants in the drug trade, at least those who survived the rigors of market competition. The passive posture of our educational system towards discouraging drug use allowed movies and tv to become the prime educators in the introduction to drug consumption, supplemented by peer pressure and street accessibility. Drug use has become the American way.

Ambitious American entrepreneurs should recognize an opportunity and consider the potential of mercantilism, an economic system that was tainted by colonialism, but may be appropriate for resurrection to aid a struggling economy. The concept of buying raw materials abroad and manufacturing finished projects at home for distribution to foreign markets could be adapted domestically. Investors could set up a hedge fund and in one application outbid the Taliban for the opium crop. Then they can cut out all the middle-men and speculators, make heroin in America and sell it at home, as well as abroad. A sufficient investment in the well-being of elected officials should insure their cooperation in facilitating legislation for a promising start-up.

Drug cartels, like certain American corporations, are ruthless in the pursuit of profit. They are uninterested in the well-being of the U.S. government, except as it affects them. They are unconcerned with the fate of the American people. This indifference from purveyors of poison to the negative consequences of drug use has expedited the expanding marketplace to include school children. Not only are we losing the war on drugs, but the virtually unrestricted diffusion of drugs is capturing new, long term markets, doing irrevocable harm to our youth. Drug use has become omnipresent in our society.

The narcotics industry has so enriched select participants that they have become a powerful oligarchy. They almost resemble traditional business empires, except they prosper from vast sales of debilitating products. They purchase legitimacy by employing legislators and lobbyists to protect and preserve their markets, regardless of ill effects on their customers. It is not illogical to assume that the illicitly funded efforts of drug lords and their supporters to maintain free market access to their products will continue indefinitely. We may not be able to stop drug use, but at least foreign contributions to the erosion of American society should be dispensed with.

Rather than allow foreigners to be the major beneficiaries of the drug trade, we should employ a dynamic initiative, promulgated by our schools, to instruct students to only consume domestically produced drugs. Schools should develop curricula that extols the benefits of domestic drug production and distribution. Entrepreneurs should be role models and be admired for earning the accruing benefits, such as mega-yachts, Picassos and luxury estates that reward Americans for their achievements, rather than foreigners. The destruction to American communities ravaged by the prevalence of drugs should at least profit Americans, who would then be required to spend their riches at home, not abroad. American entrepreneurs should be fairly taxed, so the new income stream would be allocated to alleviate fiscal burdens on the social security and health care systems.

The decay and collapse of poverty neighborhoods, with the concomitant loss of valuable youngsters to drugs, gangs and crime, can be partially ameliorated by using a larger profit margin in retail drug sales constructively. The earnings from local drug transactions spent locally would help revitalize neighborhoods, since foreign competitors would be excluded from profitable participation by protective tariffs.

This would insure the preservation and prosperity of the domestic drug industry, benefit the American economy with direct revenue sources and help rescue endangered communities.

American families should respond proactively to new market forces that will offer some consolation for the addictions and deaths of their children due to American enterprise, rather than the acquisition of toxic products from distant foreigners. The lost futures of many youngsters who might have improved our society will at least be attributable to those who speak the same language, not a foreign tongue. Drug demand will no longer benefit criminal aliens reaping offshore rewards, but will enrich our own citizens.

Schools must urgently implement the 'New Learning', and reduce classroom size to permit thorough indoctrination of all students to the virtues of home industry. Schools should produce and disseminate educational DVDs and computer games that demonstrate the superiority of domestically produced and distributed drugs, over foreign competition, in quality, price and benevolent effect on our society. Schools could offer contests seeking the best slogans to 'Produce American'. High school students who pass a test demonstrating recognition of the superiority of American drug production over foreign competition should receive a high school diploma. This will ameliorate the non-graduating problem that leaves so many youngsters without marketable skills. Now they will have a certificate that might at least give them an opportunity for better service jobs.

American industry, granted access to new capital, could innovate manufacturing techniques, pioneer scientific discoveries and utilize new social services applications that will enhance our lives, and provide affordable, reliable highs to users that will reassure the consumer market. The advertising industry could generate attractive packaging, including diverse flavors and vivid colors, for various drugs that will make the user experience more artistic. Creative copywriters and marketers could conceive appealing distribution plans for families, romantic couple specials, rugged individuals, as well as those users who can stop any time they want. A national campaign should, of course, make appropriate allowances for regional, ethnic, economic and cultural differences.

The conclusions are obvious. This revolutionary change in our dependency on foreign drug supplies cannot be implemented overnight. New industries need time to emerge. But all patriotic Americans should be encouraged to give full support to efforts that improve the way of life of our citizens. The media should publicize the efforts of the schools to improve the future of our youngsters. American owned media should endorse the grass roots attempt to enforce the right of Americans to do business in a protected environment, as we continue to build a prosperous tomorrow that will benefit the many, not just the privileged few.

Revive Our Theater Audiences

Middle class America has become liberal arts educated and culturally oriented, yet the vital qualities of critical judgment, high standards of excellence and passionate involvement are virtually non-existent in their exposure to the arts. Theater audiences, mostly nurtured by the passive media of television, or non-cognitive reactions to sports, have not developed the necessary faculties that allow positive reactions to performance. Rather than entering the theater as eager participants in a ritual that is fundamentally interactive and that mandates active emotional commitment, audiences increasingly sit back passively, observe with detachment, and except for musicals are rarely altered. Yet they frequently rise at the end for thunderous ovations of applause and bravos, patently unwarranted in proportion to the volume thereof.

Overly enthusiastic response is basically an expression of self-approval for participation in cultural affairs. The superficial cynicism or pseudo-sophistication that audiences use to cloak their ignorance of proper theater involvement becomes apparent in current trends: no one boo's performers any more. Good breeding and proper cultural behavior prohibits this crude act. Thus the actor is denied the once inalienable right of being rejected for unsatisfactory performance, the most salutary pressure for drastic improvement, or rapid departure from the profession. Audiences generally seek and approve the known and renowned, being ill-equipped to evaluate the new or obscure. From this insecurity in taste and judgment stems the inability to appreciate the developmental stages of theater, especially Off-Off Broadway, where mistakes are commonplace and technique is imperfect.

Thus audiences today are only comfortable with stars, hit shows and other socially approved phenomena, thereby avoiding the perils of personal taste and judgment, which like any other skill must be learned by trial and error. When a classic comes to Broadway it is invariably designed for one or more stars. After dozing somnolently throughout the culturally enhancing evening, the audience rises to its feet and whistles and screams bravo for almost ten minutes. It is virtually inconceivable that someone dares rise against that tidal wave of self approbation and boo a sterile, unexciting production without the stature and understanding that makes a classic meaningful. Productions lacking the energy and passion that brings classics vibrantly to life, devoid of ensemble commitment, the only practical vehicle to touch the hearts and tickle the brains of modern audiences, have become commonplace.

The demonstrable absence of effect on the audience becomes obvious when listening to the topics of conversation while they are exiting the theater. There is no emotional stir or commotion derived from the play, just mild discussions of what to do next; eat? drink? sleep? party? No passionate arousal, no reliving of exciting moments; no controversy; no moral explorations; no observations of the pertinence to life today; little or nothing beside what next?

Theater should be more than this. When audiences enter a theater without eagerness and excitement, plant themselves to endure a dose of cultural medicine, say to the actor: "Move me, despite myself", then approve without caring, we have a disease that must be urgently treated. Theater, like many other human activities, is not eternal. If it becomes meaningless, it will not endure. Although trivial compared to man's need for agriculture and engineering, theater is the most comprehensive and universal of the arts. It should address the elevation of the spirit of man, not sustain the confusions of materialism and uncertainty that assault us daily, in a complex and difficult society.

Theater audiences are college educated. Now that the colleges have become the training ground of theater professionals, they could also assume the responsibility of preparing audiences to understand the nature of theater and how to share the stage energy, which makes theater a unique experience, unlike film, where you sit back passively and spectate. Our culture is dedicated to the principle that acquiring a college diploma is necessary and just. Let the liberal arts education, which introduces a smattering of knowledge, introduce the applied art of theater appreciation for the audience.

The Decline of the American Dream

Ignorance and complacency are the great enemies preventing solutions for what is happening in our society. We go about our business, education, diversions, with insufficient thought given to the economic erosion of our nation and the growing loss of income for most of our people. Our system, created by wealthy land owners or merchants, was designed to protect the privileges of the prosperous.

The Industrial Revolution started a process that replaced humans with machines. This process continues today, with automation continuing to replace blue collar workers who were once the backbone of the nation. The loss of manufacturing jobs effectively destroyed an entire class that labored for basic comforts and the advancement of its children to a better way of life. A class that was willing to resist the abuses of the bosses. The loss of jobs and stature as breadwinners undermines the idealistic concept of parents wanting more for their children then they had, a cultural enhancement, now ending.

The great democratic experiment, more spontaneous than planned, offered virtually unlimited opportunities for those capable of adapting to their times. A working class flourished like no other time in history, producing goods and resources in hitherto unimaginable amounts. After World War II, millions of ex G.I.'s went to college, the most radical educational revolution in history. They jumped, in a few short years, to the middle class. Their children were given unprecedented luxuries, once reserved for the wealthy.

And so our nation prospered and we achieved material abundance. But we did not understand our system. As capitalists, bloated with profits, replaced more and more workers with automation, they speculated wildly. And when their financial bubbles burst, they took losses, but they destroyed the lives of millions who lost jobs, homes, savings, because they couldn't absorb the losses. Now the workers spared by automation, are facing extinction form information technology.

The few who control the bulk of our nation's wealth do not care about the sufferings of the many. They refuse to recognize the value of ordinary citizens, whose labors keep delivering food, fuel, keep transportation moving, repair planes, security systems, power supplies, yet they are being abandoned. The wealthy, like French aristas of the 18th century, are blind to who enables the flow of goods and services. The wealthy are so swollen with acquisition that they do not realize the system will collapse without maintenance. They are deaccessioning the maintainers.

We, like the dinosaur and dodo before us, have neither an inherent right to life, nor a guarantee of continuation. We have moved so far away from nature that we no longer comprehend interdependence. Greed prevails over reason. The wealthy revel in their possessions. Their ignorance and complacency of the need to sustain those who keep the machinery functioning reveals how they live: après moi, le déluge. As they doom the future of our children, they also doom the future of their children. Wealthy parents seem to be oblivious to the troubles to come. Unless the system is controlled by single old men, beyond humane concerns and compassion, there is a lack of awareness that we're all in the same boat, even though most of us are in steerage. If the boat sinks, we all go down together. We are hurtling to destruction and, so far, no one knows how to prevent the fall.

Why We Don't Need Background Checks to Purchase Guns

Many people are understandably horrified at the shootings that took place in schools, movie houses, other places once thought safe. Many citizens are outraged at the shocking violations of public safety. Some families and friends are devastated by the loss of loved ones.

However, that is no reason to abandon the laissez-faire of capitalism that has served to enrich the privileged. After all, they're not out on the streets shooting anyone. So why should we infringe their rights by intruding on their privacy with demands for distasteful registration forms when they want to acquire guns. It's up to all concerned citizens, despite moral repugnance, to accept the violent rampages that destroy our tranquility as part of the American heritage..

The Founding Fathers didn't consider individual attacks a reason for concern in the new nation. They created a wonderful document to guide a nation. Yet nowhere in the constitution does it say the right to bear arms should be denied to the mentally ill, or the criminally inclined.

If we acknowledge the validity of the pre-eminent document that defines our society, we should not inhibit access to guns for anyone. Full equality under the law should grant anyone the right to purchase firearms of choice, without interference from psychologists, monitors of proper intake of medications, or law enforcement officials.

If we deny one person the right to acquire automatic weapons, we set a precedent to deny all. The opportunity to mow down a deer with a burst of automatic fire is inherent in the fundamental values of America. The occasional disruption of lives by individual lunatics only affects a tiny percentage of our population. Majority rule mandates our tolerance of the rights of others not to be discriminated against in arbitrary and capricious background checks. Jeffersonian philosophy would not prevent equal opportunity under the law, granting all the right to acquire the firearms of choice, without the embarrassing experience of background interrogations.

Gifts of Education

The absence of theater education in grade schools and high schools, except for the privileged, along with the commensurate lack of exposure to live performance, does not build a widespread theater audience. Deadly exposure to Shakespeare in the classroom, inflicted on students without tools to grasp the language and history, makes classical theater virtually inaccessible. The school system designed to develop appropriate skills for factory labor, with the goal of job readiness in an industrial economy, cannot conceive that properly presented, theater can be practiced by anyone, regardless of talent or ability, as long as the purpose is to build self-confidence and self-esteem, rather than turn our hordes of performers.

Music and dance mandate natural talent, an early start in training, hard work, lengthy practice, intense instruction and technical mastery of their demanding arts. The lack of these requirements for students who will not pursue serious activity, provides youth an excellent opportunity in school for personal development, using theater as a mechanism. When properly encouraged, by getting up and doing things in front of others, all participants will build self-esteem and self confidence. The absence of these requirements for professional actors is one of the many factors that has contributed to the decline of classical theater, but this does not prevent the benefits of theater from enhancing youth.

Actors tend to discover theater in college or university, ten or more years after musicians and dancers began their training. Colleges took control of actor training from the professional theater in the mid-1960's. This legitimized the once disreputable profession by bestowing aspiring actors with a bachelor's degree in fine arts. The emergence of regional theaters, invariably affiliated with a well-endowed college, bewitched masses of drama students enchanted by the state-of-the-art theaters.

Enthusiastic local audiences encouraged student actors into believing their future would take place in equitable surroundings. Trained in sophisticated and protected venues, outside of the safe haven of the university, the students were woefully unfit for the harsh realities of the Off-Off Broadway theater world.

Theater education now firmly embedded in the college system, flourished academically, providing comfortable livelihoods to legions of teachers and administrators who would otherwise intermittently wander the unpaid wilderness of small theaters. The standards established by the classroom advocates were sufficient for actors intending to seek work in film or t.v. They were woefully inadequate preparations for the classical actor, who needed the same basic discipline and structure that would be the equivalent of music or dance training.

Another factor diluting serious theater was the graying of the current audience, without a new demographic audience to replace them. When adventurous classical theater lovers ventured Off-Off Broadway to see Moliere or Sophocles, they generally encountered an awkward, arbitrary updating. Deconstruction of the classics, advocated for student directors by many drama departments, invariably eliminated the class distinction of the original drama, the fundamental structure of the classics until Ibsen. This democratization removed kings, princes, barons, fatuous lovers, scheming servants and great issues, reducing the scale of drama to middle class reenactments. To add to audience travails, performances were often offered as a shouting match, rather than a dynamic, well-presented period play.

The decline of the classics is a great cultural loss to any country. But despite the disappearance of classical theater performances, that doesn't mean that theater can't play a vital role in the development of youth. Properly encouraged by aware teachers, youngsters can be enriched and better prepared for the struggles to come in a changing economy. Unlike other arts, there are no expenses. The only necessity is a sympathetic, capable teacher.

Servants of the People

The media tell us Congress is dysfunctional. Many of us accept that as an explanation of why the troubles of our nation increase.

But the reality is alarming. Congress is not dysfunctional. The hirelings of special interests are toiling away, diligently, for the benefit of those who paid for their election to national office.

When it costs 30-60 million dollars to buy a Senate seat, 2-10 million dollars to buy a House seat, careerist politicians are beholden to their funders for their current office and future aspirations.

Although our elected officials have sworn an oath to serve the nation, their obligations to their funder's interests come before the needs of the people.

It cost half a billion dollars to re-elect President Obama. Consequently it is naive to expect him to assail those funders who are disrupting our economy to the detriment of the middle class and working poor, as well as bringing long term harm to the nation. The president is also obliged to special interests.

It is our loss and the diminishment of the office that the President of the United States can not protect the voting public who elected him, millions of whom have lost jobs, homes, while the wealthy flourish.

Our education expands as we learn about the fiscal cliff, Sequestration, other economic esoterica. What new creative afflictions await us? Only the Roman Senate and the Russian Politburo were less concerned with the needs of the people. Is it conceivable that we can elect leaders not beholden to special interests, before we collapse from moral decay and privileged corruption?

Throughout history, empires and nations have collapsed or dwindled, shattering the lives and hopes of their peoples. If the wealthy cannot change some of their destructive ways, we too will become a forgotten people.

The Nature of Government

We did not learn, or have forgotten, or do not care that government was designed by the wealthy, for the use of the wealthy, even though historic documents and public pronouncements claim to include all. It is the makeup of mankind that some want more than others, especially those craving wealth and power. There is only one functional conclusion: equality is a myth. The wealthy get better medical services, better legal services, better security, better nourishment and more opportunities to acquire goods and services that they can enjoy in a protected environment.

A few accumulate a sufficiency of wealth and use some of their gain benevolently, but this is almost meaningless in the face of the vast neediness afflicting so many of our people. The wealthy, sheltered from most threats to the middle class and the poor, are oblivious to the fact that their security is dependent on the well being and capabilities of the working citizens of America. The children of the rich do not go to West Point or Annapolis, where they would learn to defend their country. Children of the wealthy do not volunteer for the military that protects their families from foreign invaders coveting their property. They do not join law enforcement and safeguard their homes from intruders. Like almost all privileged castes before them, they place themselves above the rest of the people, the needs of the nation, except as it affects them directly.

The wealthy take the protection of government for granted, and delude themselves into thinking that private security will protect them from organized attackers. The children of privilege do not serve the nation, but devour its benefits without contributing a fair share. Only the young, naïve and ignorant believe in a government of, by and for the people. When so many of the people are suffering, it is obvious that our morality is dysfunctional. Homeless children, guilty of no crime but being the offspring of disadvantaged parents, are abandoned by society. We reveal our lack of values, as well as the lack of caring by those with the means to redress this criminal abuse. Veterans, who served the nation, offering their blood and bodies, are callously discarded, while bloated parents buy Rolexes for their children of indulgence.

Despite their inequities and abuses, the wealthy should not be punished for prospering. They must be educated to understand that if they hope to continue to live securely in this country, (where else would Americans be welcome?) they must recognize their fundamental dependency on the well-being and good functioning of the people. It is imperative they learn to contribute a fair share to the well-being of the nation.

Common sense assures us it was necessary to bail out the auto companies, insurance companies, banks, to preserve the staggering economy and retain jobs. Yet at the same time it was unconscionable not to bail out the millions who lost jobs, whose homes were foreclosed, who were cruelly abandoned in their time of need. We cannot be a great society when millions of our people go hungry. We must better prepare the mechanism of government to serve all the people and remind the privileged of noblesse obligé.

Cassandra: A Character Study

Cassandra is a minor, but vital character in Aeschylus' drama, Agamemnon. She informs the audience of the forthcoming death of Agamemnon, as well as herself, precipitating the action to come. Presumably the audience knows what's coming, since it is a tragedy. The challenge to the director is to make the prophecy of imminent death theatrically dramatic to an audience visually saturated by the incredibly sophisticated imagery of film and tv.

In order to construct the emotional involvement of the audience in a scene that is critically important, Cassandra must compel a range of feelings. This can be facilitated by the chorus, who can express qualities of scorn, derision, mockery, pity, for the possessed woman. The actor, by creating tension before, during and after prophecy, completes the stage requirements for furthering the action.

The source of developing the depth of character necessary for Cassandra to evoke tragic awareness is in the pre-history of the Iliad and the myth of the House of Atreus. The director and actor should presuppose that the audience may be familiar with the tale of Troy, and possibly even the play itself. They should assume the audience will not know the myth of Apollo and Cassandra, which could be the key to initiating the foundation of constructing the character. Cassandra, a young royal princess (12-14?) of the house of Priam of Troy, is desired by the god Apollo. She agrees to have sex with him, if he'll give her the gift of Prophecy. He does. Then she mocks him and refuses to keep her part of the bargain. He can't take back his gift, so he curses her with not being believed.

This is where the actor's work begins. This once privileged personage is now an embarrassment, a demented creature, possessed of madness, yet still a beloved member of the royal house. All these qualities must be examined and included in the character. The curse began before the Trojan War, which lasted for ten years, followed by the capture and destruction of the city. Then Cassandra was awarded as a slave to Agamemnon and presumably was his bedmate during their return to Argos. By building the character's emotional life for at least ten years before she comes on stage, the actor may arrive with a three dimensional persona that will stir the audience's emotion.

The exploration of pre-character should not be a day to day diary, or a chronicle. There should be some invented salient facts or experiences that will lead to the tormented emotional state of a character alienated from the world around her. It is vital to understand that Cassandra has been disbelieved many times. She has probably been treated as a privileged, demented member of the royal household, yet was considered harmless.

Cassandra surely prophesized the fall of Troy, which largely had to have been laughed at. The inner torment at being mocked and pitied would be a constant. It is useful to be aware that prophecy is a 'divine' gift, not an act of reason, therefore, the prophet will be possessed/transformed, while in a state of inspiration.

A physical transformation when in the state of prophecy must be carefully created so as not to be contrived, grotesque, silly, etc. Any implausible quality that might make the character unbelievable to the audience must be eliminated. The complication for the director is how to get the chorus, whatever format to use them is selected, to sustain disbelief in the prophecy, despite the fact that the audience knows it's true. Since the curse of disbelief is on Cassandra, she must be convincing, or the scene will be contrived and the audience involvement with the play will deflate.

Of course very few actors will have the opportunity to play Cassandra, at least in a serious theater setting. Yet the same general outline of character development can be applicable to other roles. Create who you are, then you will be, of course pre-supposing you have the talent and skills to be.

The Abandonment of America

As the American empire declines, the wealthy are feasting, buying Rothkos at auction, gloating over clever investments, amassing offshore bank accounts. They do not seem aware that when the American hegemony collapses, Western Europe will inevitably follow, inextricably linked by countless ties, political, economic, values. After the fall of Western civilization, and it need not be sacked by barbarian hordes, just dwindled to join poverty nations, thereafter struggling to survive in a harsh world, most of which hates America.

If they even think that far ahead, where do privileged Americans hope to withdraw to? Asia, Africa, Europe and the Mid-East are too dangerous. South America, rife with envy, anti-Americanism, and nationalism as a prevailing attitude, characteristics that make the climate inhospitable. The Caribbean is the remaining illusion. Unless the émigrés have a large, sophisticated, well-equipped, well trained, well-paid, private army, island life will at best be insecure, at worst, a place of constant threat of attack, looting, murder.

Unfortunately for all of us, the wealthy suffer from political blindness and historical ignorance. They do not realize that they still live in the most secure country in the world. Yet they sit back as it declines, unknowing, unwilling or unable to apply resources to prevent the fall that would insure their future demise. If they are just a cabal of old men, with little concern for tomorrow, there is little hope for their understanding that our fate is bound together. Wealthy families with children should realize the future well-being of their children is completely dependant on the well-being and stability of the nation.

The working people who keep this country running, air controllers, first responders, snow removal for highways, all the vital jobs that keep the planes flying, maintain the roads, provide the provisions and luxury items that allow a lavish lifestyle, give the same basic services to most Americans. We share the roads, the airports, the food chains, so many things that inextricably bind all of us together. But the wealthy don't perceive that their survival lifeboats won't float without cooperation from the crew.

The privileged apparently do not see that when the police cease to function, no one is safe. The private estates, guarded compounds, protected enclaves are only preserved by the rule of law. In the absence of order, angry, hungry, frightened mobs will inevitably select targets of luxury, whether in city or countryside. When the wealthy can't summon law enforcement, the National Guard, invoke martial law to protect their property, they will not survive the inroads of violent, desperate people.

Some brighter wealthy persons learned one lesson from the past. In times of disaster, the wealthy fled with what they could carry, jewels, rolled up paintings, other easily transported valuables. So they diversified their wealth, much of it abroad, presuming they found safe havens. But when abroad becomes unreachable,

international law and order may no longer protect lawful claims. Then foreign holdings are at best vulnerable to seizure by amoral bankers, whose normal business activity frequently evades legal procedures. The message should be clear. The only long-term security for all, wealthy and poor alike, is in a secure homeland.

Unlike the brave blind, who venture out into the hazards of a dark world and build a viable life, the privileged are not seeing that their future in the nation that nurtured them and their children is endangered by their obstinately personifying "Aprés moi, le deluge". It is a fervent hope that they come to their senses before it's too late and recognize that all will drown if the ship of state sinks.

The Progress of Capitalism

In the 1930's, many Americans still lived on small farms, hard-working people struggling to eke a livelihood from the land, like peasant farmers for thousands of years before them. However, these farmers were different than their forebears. They believed in the Constitution of the United States, even when it didn't work for them. They took pride in their individual holdings and believed they were the equals of anyone. That their children, weary of the backbreaking daily toil, yearned for the life of the cities, puzzled the simple parents, who valued their independence, despite the terrible toll on their bodies and souls. The owners of America, through glamorous movies and magazines, facilitated the lure of restless youngsters into giving up the land and seeking a more appealing life in the cities.

At the same time, militant unions were defying management, with hard won confidence in their worth. Their willingness to fight scabs and goons for better pay and working conditions, alarmed the wealthy owners, always intent on acquiring more wealth and power. Labor was not only the biggest expense of businesses and factories, but the biggest headache, with demands for more of a share of the profits for their efforts. Peasant revolts were never appreciated by the masters.

World War II solved many problems for the ruling class. Millions of young men were taken from the farms and factories, and not only exposed to war, but were shown a bigger world. The massive industrial production of planes, ships, vehicles and all the other implements of war summoned millions to war plants, to produce what was needed to fight a global war. Women were included for the first time in hitherto exclusive masculine work environs, which gave them a heady taste of life outside the home. When women performed as well as the men they were further empowered.

The enormous economic growth spurred by the war created a new element of society. The men who came home from military service didn't go back to farms and factories, they went to college, paid for by the G.I. Bill. And they became doctors, lawyers, accountants, business men, leaving behind manual toil. And they found a new prosperity that included homes, cars, appliances, vacations, luxuries barely imagined in the past. And their children grew up with comfort, rather than the strenuous labor that toughened their forebears, made them desperate for change in their way of life, made them willing to fight for improvement.

And the offspring of the new middle-class took comforts for granted. And their indulgent parents, who had built new lives, new interests, neglected the moral education of their children and did not teach them fundamental values. So the children of television nurturing resented efforts by school authorities to regulate behavior. Instead of following what they considered obsolete codes of conduct, they began to 'turn on, tune in, drop out'.

The unions were still strong and there were still many small farms, so automation began another offensive against human workers. And the cities grew, swollen with populations dependent on a sophisticated system of supply and demand, for survival. Then an expanding war in far off Asia further drained the farms and factories, emptied the ghettos of angry youth resentful of constricted lives. When these reluctant warriors came back from overseas, they were not welcomed by the children of privilege, who had stayed home making merry and partying, while less fortunate youngsters bled on hostile shores.

As automation advanced technically and removed more and more hands-on jobs, manual and applied skills were devalued. Engineers became invisible, while lawyers captured the public eye. Liberal arts liberally attracted millions of youth who were ill-equipped for the tasks of building and maintaining a society. They were encouraged to participate in education that did not educate young minds to grapple with the issues of their times, or prepare them to acquire the tools to improve their society.

While thousands of colleges absorbed millions of youngsters, the unions were depleted by what seemed to many the inevitable replacement of man by machine. The blue collar class, once respected for vital skills and services, was now sneered at by the college educated. To fix a toilet was no longer a passport to a better life for one's children. Almost everyone accepted the premise of a college education as the valid route to well-being. But this socially approved route that nurtured millions, who acquired their degrees. the promised passports to prosperity, discovered painfully that it no longer led to good jobs, advancement, comforts, security.

When the bubble of prosperity burst, it cost millions of families jobs, homes, savings, hope for the future. There no longer existed a capable class able to fight for the continuation of the rights of workers. Instead, the former sustainers of our nation and their vulnerable children were confronted with a meager future, with no possibility of college education as a mechanism to change it. Now the masters were able to remove the privileges of the liberally educated, who had become superfluous in a rapidly growing technocracy. The amalgamation of wealth had triumphed over the concept of a fair share for all. Once again, greed prevailed, as the few reveled, while the many suffered.

Petty Literary Money Grubbers

The two most prominent non-performing arts are painting (a genre term that includes all the fine art forms) and writing. An art gallery is a vital business that links the artist to the buyer. Almost all galleries are for profit, paying the artist a percentage of sales. The more well known and desired the artists, they naturally get a larger percentage. The other type of galleries are either not-for-profit, or collectives, with different structures of remuneration. Some artists feel that galleries take an inordinate share of earnings. Many artists resent the semi-closed world of galleries that do not readily accept new artists. This is a relatively traditional arts business, since artists ceased being artisans in the second half of the 19th century and acquired agents, rather than patrons to promote their work. Of course, except for dealers in old masters, a gallery's selection of artists to represent is purely subjective.

Writing, until the advent of electronic publishing, was not entirely dissimilar to the art business. Publishing houses issued the books of their writers and paid them royalties. Invariably, except for successful commercial fiction writers, it became difficult for serious writers to earn a livelihood by their craft. This certainly urged many of them to seek refuge in hospitable academic environments that offered a modicum of security and captive audiences. Then came the proliferation of emags.

In an amusing historical note, in the 1970's, the eruption of Off- Off Broadway theater ventures allowed, for the first time, inexperienced youngsters to start their own companys with little or no professional or business know-how. At this time, the average life span of a new theater company was three to four months. This confirmed the good sense of the National Endowment of the Arts that required a group to be in existence for at least two years before requesting funding. Then they would face the standard of artistic excellence, and if they were denied grants, they believed it was for not belonging to an old boy's (or girl's) theater network.

Then the children of the publishing arts multiplied. And no longer had to serve demanding, underpaid apprenticeships at traditional publishing houses to learn the publishing business. While everyone else is struggling in America in the twenty first century of economic malaise for the diminishing middle class, the liberal arts college degree finally had its era of utility. Formerly, the most useless preparation for the future, now the lib-arts grad could use simple computer skills, simple art skills, simple writing skills to start a magazine. By 2015 there were over 5,000 emags, most of them run by well-meaning, but ill-prepared dabblers.

Many of the nouveau arrivistes pressured their writers to subscribe to their magazines, thus hoping to pay for their new business. At the same time, tens of thousands of new writers, urgent for publication, collaborated with their new publisher by paying for subscriptions. In the 1930's, if a writer self-published, or was published by a vanity press, it was either a joke, or an embarrassment. Now this phenomenon, a torrent of writers and a host of epublishers, formed a low-yield symbiosis. This was a union of true ignorance. The publishers believed they were entitled to money from the writers. The writers thought it was normal to support the magazines that published them.

The worst offenders in this pay to play arena are the contest sponsors. Even the well-established, supposedly responsible literary magazines and the university publications reap income by offering contests with an entry fee, that attracts participants hoping for recognition far more then prize money. Many of them also yearn for the cash. The practice of charging writers to be published is unprincipled, exploitive and deleterious in the effect on the mentalities of writers and publishers alike.

In an era of dominant visuals in entertainment, and unrestricted access to the internet, the performing arts are fading. Painting (including all the other facets of fine art) has become so diverse in form and technique, that it is no longer accessible to the basic culture seeker. Writing has expanded more then any other art form because it requires the least skill, the least investment in materials. Great writing has faded away in the publishing climate of mass market sales. Throughout history, culture has arisen and departed, often linked ot the life and death of empires. It is no tragedy that opera, ballet, classical music, classical theater are fading away in our society. Change in cultural values is inevitable, despite the reluctance of certain participants to accept the new reality.

It is appropriate for writers to realize that they should be paid for their work, rather then paying to be published. There should be some kind of standard to determine remuneration. Certainly the merit of the work should be considered. The reality is that very few of us know the difference between good and bad art, let alone good and bad writing. Liberal arts graduates, deluded into assuming they are educated, do not comprehend that if they want to be publishers, it's like any other arts venture. It's a business. If someone wants to be a publisher, they should learn how to finance their business, not expect to be funded by writers. Writers should learn not to participate in publication's allurements, where they pay to be in print. It is improbable that either group will have the common sense to reverse their erroneous behavior patterns, but they should certainly be made aware of the impropriety of payment for publication.

An amusing afterthought. In semi-professional and community theater, where there is scarcely any money to pay artists, musicians insist: 'Musicians must be paid'.

The Mental Health of the Nation

A society might be considered clinically insane when it approves the sales of alcoholic beverages, tolerates the sales of illegal drugs, then tries to legally ban the sale of large sugar content soda containers.

It is a testament to our times when we confuse unhealthy beverages, with toxic substances. However harmful excess sugar intake may be, it pales next to the consumption of liquor or narcotics, with a by product of drunken driving and drug overdoses.

Is the anti-sugar campaign a sincere concern for the health of our citizens, or is it a sneaky distraction from more disturbing problems? When we consider all the daily threats to our existence that seem to be multiplying, we might wonder why a mayor leads a crusade against sugar.

The Nature of Social Distraction

Hide the cigarettes! After all, temptation can not be resisted, once we espy the glittering packets of allurement, leading to deleterious consumption.

And while we react to another dicta from a mayor vitally concerned with our well-being, 20,000 homeless children are suffering in the homeless system, through no fault of their own. They are the innocent victims of their parent's problems.

But they are hidden away from public scrutiny and officialdom doesn't care about their fate. Some of them, if properly nurtured, could enrich our struggling society with their talent. Forget them though. It's too complex, too difficult to solve their problems. So hide them away.

Make us think about hiding cigarettes. That's easy. Some will go along. Some will object. After all, public debate is good. Except when it conceals violations of the rights of life, liberty and the pursuit of happiness.

The Decline of Snod

In the Hegalian tradition of philosophy there is a concept relative to the rise and fall of civilization. Purely for the sake of science we are interested in Hegal's "antithesis", which would be the temporary decline of a culture preceding a glorious renaissance. We shall use the example of the waning culture of the decadent land of Snod to question the wisdom of Hegal, and express the fear that even a dedicated and capable leadership could not salvage a promising techno-industrial empire, bankrupted and beggared by it's own greedy citizens..

Looking back at the childhood of Phineas Bosgood jr, no one would imagine that he was destined in later years to hold the highest office in the venerable government of Snod; that of the All-High Clod of Snod. Despite the accomplishments of his father, Phineas Bosgood, sr, who after holding various important positions in the government of Snod, was elected to the highest office, the All-High Clod, Junior's beginnings were undistinguished. He was of average intelligence, a distressing condition in a society already afflicted with Dumbing Down Syndrome, (DDS).

Junior's educational career was mediocre, characterized by barely passing grades in college and participation in alcohol and drug consumption, a frequent activity of many young Snodians, who were completely oblivious to their responsibilities to their nation and the future. Unlike the All-High Clod, who followed Senior, Junior performed military service, all-be-it, removed from any war zone. But he became a jet fighter pilot, thereby partially refuting the suspicions of being an early victim of DDS.

Then, in what many Snodians believed to be a veritable, although minor miracle, Junior was transformed, and became a local government leader, exhibiting piety and sincerity. Then in what many considered a greater miracle, despite the disputed results, he was elected to the highest office in the land. His oligarch manipulators, interested only in profits from their investments and continued well-being, were unconcerned with the collapse of Snodian industry, the decay of public institutions and a crushing national debt that condemned future Snodians to poverty and deprivation. But the oligarchs needed to divert the people while they milked the system for the last bit of gain, regardless of the harm done to Snod and the Snodians.

Therefore, according to tried and true Snodian tradition, whenever the way of life of the privileged was threatened, they resorted to a time honored solution; an appropriate foreign war. This would be presented to the public as a democratic crusade against a particularly distasteful group of foreigners who threatened the stability of the world order, menaced their neighbors, practiced ethnic cleansing, or in the bestest ever justification for military action, were seeking weapons of mass destruction.

In an age when the media are owned by those who may not have the best interests of the people as their prime motive, the access to information by the general public is extremely limited. In fact, Snodians have been allowed until recently to accumulate so much in the way of goods and services, that except when it affects them personally, they tend to accept the information from the media at face value, and ignore any questionable activities of their government that they are told doesn't concern them.

When a clod, with virtually unlimited power becomes righteous about issues that are conceived to disguise rapacious economic imperialism, promulgated by military force, a hopeful society is betrayed and precipitated to an undesirable future. In a world still characterized by nationalism, a Saddam Hussein, as a vaunted hegemon, is the recipient of unmitigated suspicion and hatred. Snodians, persuaded by their leaders and the media that they are supporting a just cause, are as much victims as their targets of external aggression. A people once promised a better life than their parents, have been abandoned by the oligarchs, with the tacit consent of their government, as far back as the 'sixties', when capital was moved to industry abroad, leaving us the rust belt and other depressed areas.

The Clod is an excellent figurehead to receive our criticisms and grievances, but he is merely a tool of ruthless, amoral masters, whose only concern is for their accumulation and maintenance of money and power. The evils of the land of Snod, committed in the manipulation of private interests, are abusive and exploitive. However, who should lead us to a better world? France? Russia? Egypt? China? Is there a nation less guilty than Snod of international violations of the law? Is it possible that better the Clod we have, than one we know not of? As Iran sinks back to the seventh century, except in armaments, how will Snod crumble?

Contemporary historians, especially the glib and clever, who are sheltered in their secure fortresses of academia and do not have to struggle for their daily bread, are quick to condemn our Clod as well as Snod for their crimes against humanity. However, these sheltered snipers have nothing better to offer and only add to the leaks in the lifeboats of survival. As we submerge with decay, whether in gradual decline, to be followed by rapid collapse, the most obvious diagnosis of our situation is the total lack of wisdom in Snod for problem solving, domestic or foreign. Our future looks grim without meaningful change that will improve our prospects for tomorrow.

www.ingramcontent.com/pod-product-compliance
Lightning Source LLC
LaVergne TN
LVHW091709190726

843493LV00001B/224